The Hush House Affair

A Case Of Creative Destruction

(No, It's Not A 'No -Tell' Motel)
Reference: Page 90

Richard J. Reilly

DEDICATION

To the memory of Major General Bobby Bond, whose operational experience, knowledge of Department of Defense Procurement practices and bold initiative made this program possible.

CONTENTS

ILLUSTRATIONS

ILLUSTRATIONS

PREFACE

The story is born in conflict, but the end-game results in a $49 million contract with the U.S. Air Force. It is a story of 'Creative Destruction,' a term, popularized by Austrian/American Economist and Harvard Professor, Joseph Schumpeter, to describe the process by which old products are replaced by new devices, ideas or methods. A more mundane expression of this idea is the 'buggy whip' analog: A whip for one's buggy is unnecessary when it is powered by a gasoline engine, and an industry disappears.

The "Hush House Affair" chronicles a nearly four-year odyssey that spans five countries and replaces the historical use of water for cooling aircraft noise suppressors with an air-cooling technique. It is a head-on collision: Water cooling, with its columns of black smoke, acid rain and other operational undesirables, becomes environmentally untenable. Air cooling eliminates these negatives, and significant cost savings result as a bonus. In addition, the lawsuits brought by noise and acid rain are eliminated. Air as a cooling agent wins handily for many reasons.

The plot could be that of an adventure novel. The protagonists engage in an explosive conflict on first meeting but combine their talents to engage in a classic Schumpeterian conflict with the U.S. government: One industry is destroyed and is replaced by a new enterprise, producing a superior, environmentally more benign product, under a government contract.

The battle is not easily won.

traditional industries fight back. Government agencies, steeped in comfortable operational and business relationships, indulge in an internecine rivalry. The new technology is often threatened but is rescued by fortuitous and almost mysterious means. When the contract is finally consummated, one of my principal adversaries approached me and extended his hand, saying,

"Hey, no hard feelings. It was your general against our general, and your general won." He didn't understand how his team lost. You will.

I hope you enjoy the chronological account of this odyssey.

Richard Reilly

May 2018

ACKNOWLEDGMENTS

I owe a deep appreciation to the many characters who appeared inexplicably, when most needed, to fend off disaster during the nearly four years it took to drive the Hush House Program to success.

I am especially grateful to Peter Garrison who contributed so much time for discussions and advice on the preparation of the manuscript.

The Hush House Affair

Other books by the Author

Tell Me A Story
46 Short stories from five continents

Marketing To The Government
College Course textbook with Keith Akkre

1

Introduction

*Sometimes life serves up a curve-ball you know you should
let pass by, but you swing at it anyway.*

* * *

E ngineering is pretty much a linear profession: A problem is
defined and analyzed using physical laws and mathematics.
A validating device or experiment is built to test the
hypothesis. The resulting data leads to a conclusion: an improved
device, a refined experiment or a written report, and onward to the
next problem. Mix this process with politics, bureaucratic rules, or
internecine disputes between organizations fighting for their interests,
or their very lives, and the skills required are very different from
classical engineering. The trajectory then meanders. There is no

longer a straight line between the beginning and the end. The old cliche about 'herding cats' may be appropriate, but perhaps a better parallel is trying to refold a cheap, plastic raincoat into its original travel package.

I got into the Hush House Program almost by accident. It was a techno-political odyssey that lasted more than four years and changed the way the U.S. Air Force conducted ground testing of jet airplanes and engines. The program resulted in a $49 million contract, which required the manipulation of the U.S. Budget for the 1980 Fiscal Year. Before the contract was signed, I made more than 2,000 telephone calls and traveled over 150,000 miles, in five countries. The successful outcome was the result of unusual efforts by many people as a result of fortuitous intersections and events. The contract was the largest ever awarded by the U.S. Air Force for ground support equipment up to that time.

What Is A Hush House?

Individual Muffler

By way of orientation it might be well to illustrate what a Hush House is. The name was assigned by the original builder of these facilities, Granges-Nyby, a Swedish company. Jet airplanes are noisy things. By the mid 1970s, ground testing of aircraft and engines was regarded as a nuisance, as opposed to a symbol of national power and pride, and mufflers, of some sort, became required by popular demand.

The typical muffler consisted of a large, acoustically treated pipe that received the jet exhaust products, quieted and cooled them. To keep the sound from escaping at the entrance of the pipe, it was fitted with a large box that contained only the tail of the aircraft. The entrance to the attenuating pipe was usually of cruciform shape, fitted around the tail surfaces and rear fuselage of an aircraft, and all the contacting edges were padded to prevent damage to the relatively fragile surfaces. In addition, a feeble attempt was made to stop the high frequency noise from escaping forward by hanging form-fitting boxes over the aircraft's inlets. To achieve a close fit, both the front and rear enclosures required a different design for each individual aircraft-type in the Air Force inventory. To keep the pipe from destruction by the exhaust flame, cooling-water was injected into the jet efflux in huge quantities, many hundreds of gallons per minute.

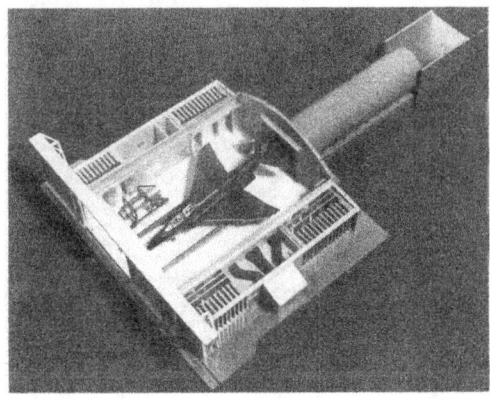

Hush House

The Hush House is different: It encloses the entire airplane, and utilizes air-cooling. Engine noise is trapped by acoustic baffles along the sides of the hangar, while cooling air is permitted free passage into the interior.

The Hush House's appearance was timely. Environmentally, spraying water into the exhaust products of jet engines became untenable. It produced plumes of dark, black smoke and sulfuric acid rain as it mixed with hot residual sulfur in the burning fuel.

Politically, the Hush House introduced serious tensions within the operational structure of the Air Force. It eliminated ongoing design and building of acoustic mufflers specifically fitted to individual aircraft. Moving these test facilities from base to base with changing deployments of aircraft, would no longer be required. Millions of dollars could be saved annually. The downside of all this: The Air Force had an entire logistic organization at Wright Field dedicated to the design, building, moving and repairing of the custom-fitted mufflers, worldwide. They weren't having anything to do with the universal hangar that would put them out of business.

Bringing about this transformation was a long and difficult process, with many inexplicable twists and turns. The book recounts this four-year odyssey in chronological detail, but a short version of the story was published contemporaneously by "Corporate Report" magazine, an Upper Midwest "Business Week" of sorts. While the writer, Don Larson, captures some of my personal frustrations along the way, he gives little credit to the nearly providential appearance of many people who were key to the final contractual success. Nevertheless, his summary article serves well as a road map for a difficult four-year journey.

*   *   *

PERSONAL PERSPECTIVE   *Don W. Larsen*

Looking for a Fat

Government Contract?

Let's assume for a moment that you're the head of a small manufacturing company doing about $7 million in annual sales. You're pitching for a very large contract from a single customer, a $45-million contract – about six times your present annual volume. The customer is the U.S. Air Force, and it's impressed. Negotiations are conducted, you convince the people involved you can produce the product, and the contract is awarded to you.

Sounds simple, doesn't it?

Well, a Twin Cities firm recently went through this very exercise, with the same happy result, but it was far from simple. When Aero Systems Engineering, Inc., St. Paul, signed a $45-million Air Force contract for 25 elaborate shelters in which to test jet aircraft and engines, the event marked the conclusion of an almost unbelievable tale of battling in bureaucratic jungles. It should be a good warning to any small company seeking government business.

A knowledgeable independent consultant, Richard J. Reilly of St. Paul, deserves much of the credit for Aero Systems' eventual success in getting the contract. Over the years Reilly has learned how to effectively cut government red tape, but the Aero Systems job proved that even an expert can be, at times, overwhelmed in dealing with bureaucrats.

The Aero Systems-Air Force saga started more than four years ago. In October 1976, when Olov Muten, chairman and chief executive of the small St. Paul firm, decided he wanted that Air Force contract and was ready to bet his company on the outcome, he hired Reilly to fight for it, even though Reilly warned him there was less than a one-percent chance a firm as small as Aero Systems could land such a whopping job.

The contract was awarded to Aero Systems 39 months later. Reilly devoted most of that time to the project, traveling more than 150,000 miles in five countries and making more than 2,000 long distance phone calls. Bureaucrats in Washington still scratch their heads over such a large award going to such a small company. The $45-million award is the largest single support-equipment contract in Air Force history, and Aero Systems is the smallest company to get any type of large government job. Yet, even after the contract was awarded, the complications weren't over. There was still another nine months involved in fighting protests from those representing firms which had lost the job.

But the choice was far from capricious. Success in landing the contract can be attributed to three factors:
• Aero Systems is one of the few companies in the world with the expertise to build a complex shelter in which to safely and efficiently test a jet aircraft engine.
• Muten, Robert Lucas, Aero Systems president, and others at the company, had the faith and patience to keep plugging along during the months when it seemed that the frustrations weren't worth the prospect of losing the company.
• Reilly's experience in dealing with the complexities inside the bewildering maze, where government contracts are awarded was the key to convincing military authorities that Aero Systems could actually deliver if it got the project.

Reilly's credentials are impressive. An aeronautical engineer with extensive graduate work in gas dynamics, compressible fluid flow and supersonic inlets for aircraft gas turbines, Reilly not only understands the technical aspects involved but has a background in the business end of this field, as well. He has been an engineer and research scientist for several Twin Cities companies, including General Mills, Honeywell, and Rosemount Research Center. He holds 15 patents, has written more than 20 technical papers, and has been a guest lecturer at several universities in the U.S. and Europe.

One of Reilly's first hurdles in winning the Air Force contract was to convince the military authorities of the superiority of Aero Systems' air-cooled testing principles over the water-cooled system the Air Force has been using. Air Force brass told him the system used by the military was satisfactory, even though the technicians in the field admitted to Reilly they were having immense problems. Hundreds of meetings with Pentagon officials and Air Force officers at installations around the country and even in several foreign nations were necessary before the real selling job could begin.

Many of the meetings were major disappointments to Reilly and some were attended only by Reilly himself. Once, for example, Reilly had lined up an important session in Washington, D.C., with several Air Force equipment and logistics people. When he arrived in the nation's capital, after making the arrangements by long distance calls from St. Paul earlier, he went directly to the meeting. Only one official showed up, and he had no authority to take any action. The others had all canceled out because of the "extreme" weather. It was 13 degrees above zero in Washington. It was well below zero when Reilly left St. Paul.

Even getting the necessary information from the military to comply with its own instructions proved difficult. On one occasion, Reilly was told he couldn't get the life-cycle cost data he requested without using the Freedom of Information Act, a tedious process. He finally got the data after a lengthy delay.

Midway through the three-year struggle to get the contract, Reilly was told he needed an Air Force research and development program to get a National Stock Number before the operations people could consider purchase of the equipment. The research and development people said he didn't qualify for it because the Aero Systems equipment was an existing product and not eligible for an R&D program. Catch 22!

Slowly, methodically, Reilly removed one roadblock after another. The winning of the contract has cost Aero Systems hundreds of thousands of dollars, but it has been worth it. The company is already involved in fulfilling the terms of the contract. Manufacturing facilities are being constructed in Crockett, Texas, and soon 150 workers will be constructing the 25 testing facilities.

Companies in this area which might be considering seeking government contracts to beef up their operations should give serious thought to the problems encountered by Aero Systems. It's a routine procedure for firms such as Honeywell, Control Data or Univac, but for a small or medium-sized firm, the prospects of doing work on a large scale for the government are mighty slim. CR

Don W. Larson is senior editor of CORPORATE REPORT and publisher of the Business Newsletter.+

2

Hush House: The Cast of Characters

*The success of the Hush House program was the result of
dedicated and often risky efforts by many people who
appeared, almost providentially, when needed most.*

*   *   *

An appreciation of the Hush House story may be enhanced
by meeting some of the people involved. More than any
other endeavor I've been involved with, the strange
appearance of key people, when most needed or most unwanted, was
an unusual characteristic of the program. These people, their interests, abilities and failings, were essential to the ultimate, successful
conclusion of this effort. Skip this section if you like; the continuity

remains, but knowing the people makes it more interesting.

Olof Muten

Olof Muten was the Chairman of the Board of Aero Systems Engineering. A native of Sweden, Olof was the stereotypical Scandinavian: tall, graying blond hair and penetrating blue eyes. The Hush House Program is as much Olof's story as mine, but the story nearly died in my first contact with him. To a great extent, understanding the program means understanding Olof. Olof was a very proud man, however, he could display some rough edges and a thuggish side when challenged. Once he decided he liked you, however, you could do no wrong.

It wasn't long before he revealed his background. Born of proletarian ancestry, he joined the Swedish Military after completing a collegiate curriculum. He advanced quickly into the officer corps, where he soon found himself outgunned by his peers because he lacked the personal finances required to meet the social obligations of a Swedish Military Officer. However, he made many acquaintances with people who became high-level captains of Swedish Industry: the presidents of Saab and Volvo, among many others, and more important to the current story, the President and Managing Director of Granges-Nyby, Ole Lund.

Resigning his commission and nearly penniless, he emigrated to the United States in 1956, taking up residence in the YMCA in Philadelphia. In 1960 he retired for the first time, from the Vice Presidency of Marketing for the Sunbeam Corporation, a large, respected manufacturer of small electric appliances.

Scraping together his 'small change,' in the time of a 'down' stock market, he bought a seat on the New York Stock Exchange and rode the stock boom of the 1960s to truly independent wealth. When we met, he owned a large industrial food catering service, which served hot meals, for lunches and work-breaks, from trucks routed through out Eastern Pennsylvania and Western Delaware.

It was a tough business, Mafia dominated by heavy-handed un-ions that were quick to threaten bodily harm to interlopers. Olof was equal to the task, and it gave him some entertainment besides counting his money. Dealing with the Mafia elements may have honed his thuggish tendencies.

Olof was a very intense man. His only recreational relief was de-rived from a three-masted schooner, which he kept on the Baltic Sea and riding to the hounds on the estates of the elite in Delaware and Pennsylvania, where he had a large gentleman's farm. He was on a first-name basis with the DuPonts and other families chronicled in the society pages of the day, but more of that later.

As a potential employee, he judged me by only one question:

"What is your net worth?" While I could not measure up to him in that department, he regarded my answer as acceptable, probably because we had no debts. We developed a very trusting business relationship, where I could make decisions and speak for him, know-ing my words would be backed by both funding and action. Several times, unable to reach him for an urgent decision, I took an over-night airplane, only to call him in the morning from Germany or England and say,

"Olof, I spent another thousand dollars of your money last night."

"Good," he'd reply, "I'm sure it was necessary."

Lars Broberg

Lars Broberg was an engineer to his very heart but not a very good businessman. As a result, shortly before I met him, the firm he founded, Aero Systems Engineering, had been acquired by a Swedish firm. Granges-Nyby took possession of the company, for non-pay-ment of bills owed for stainless steel used in construction of engine test cells in Europe. Lars was intimidated by his newly acquired Swedish overlords.

Lars had an intuitive understanding of physical principles, and as a designer of specialized jet engine test cells and test equipment he was a perfectionist. On one occasion I saw him, accompanied by a welder and a painter, modify an engine thrust stand that was already on a flatbed truck with its engine idling, awaiting shipment to a customer. Lars simply couldn't finish anything; there was always an improvement to be made. He was a poster man for the expression,

"Perfection is the enemy of pretty darn good."

Major Ted Capps

Ted Capps was a desk officer in the Pentagon, perhaps one of the nastiest jobs in the Air Force. In addition to the business of managing major Air Force programs, these men, who flew desks, were at the mercy of the Congress. Frequently, often several times a week during budget crises, they would be called to deal with what were known as 'Suspenses,' requirements from legislators to answer in detail the 'whys' and status of programs under their control. These often occurred late in the day, with the response required by the following morning. Usually, this meant he worked until midnight. His wife, who also worked somewhere in the Pentagon, would then sleep in their car until Ted finished with his congressional duties. He was ultimately responsible for our being able to successfully complete the Hush House Program for Aero Systems.

Major General Bobby Bond

General Bond was one of the many people who fortuitously appeared in my life at a critical time. I met him when I suffered a 'busted' meeting at the Pentagon, as weather interfered with people arriving at work on time. I wandered into the reception area of an office complex, looking for one of my scheduled meeting's participants. He had not yet made an appearance, but I heard a voice from another office, which opened into the same reception area.

"C'mon in" it said. As I stepped into the office, a genial character extended his hand.

"I'm Bobby Bond. Nobody seems to be working today so sit

down, let's talk. What are you doing here?" Thus began a major key to the entire Hush House program.

I never saw General Bond after that day. Shortly thereafter he was killed in the crash of an alleged prototype airplane, but the circumstances were all secret. A 24-hour guard was set around the crash site in the Sierra Nevada mountains. A cover story was concocted to explain Bond's demise. He was likely flying a captured, Russian Mig-29, but the story became entangled with the then-secret 'Have Blue' prototypes. The latter was likely cover to confuse Russian intelligence regarding our knowledge of the Mig.

Paul Dembling Esq.

Paul was a Washington, D.C. attorney who was, before retirement, Chief Counsel for NASA and later for the General Accounting Office (GAO). With his deep knowledge of the inner workings of government at many levels, he was able to guide me through the final chaos of dealing with the legal protests to the Hush House contract lodged with the GAO.

Sgts. Chesters and Morris

Sergeants Chesters & Morris

Sergeant Chesters ran the Hush House test facility at Royal Air Force Base Coningsby, about 150 miles north of London. His durable enthusiasm and cooperation made it possible for us to complete a series of tests within the time allotted to me by the British Royal

Air Force. He was extremely well-read and the only person I've ever known to curse in Shakespearean English.

Sergeant Morris, his sidekick, made things happen when problems seemed without recourse. In the middle of the night he risked a court martial to save a crucial set of tests.

Senior Master Sergeants Graham & Nettles

Sr. M. Sgts. Graham & Nettles

Senior Master Sergeants are the soul of the U.S. Air Force. They often have the complete trust of their high-ranking officers. General Bond, during that fateful morning in Washington, D.C., told me the key to making the Hush House program click was to get the cooperation of Graham and Nettles. At the time, Graham was stationed at U.S. Air Force Headquarters Europe, in Ramstein, W. Germany and Nettles was stationed in the Headquarters of the Tactical Air Command, at Langley Field Virginia. Many times, during the the program, Graham and Nettles were consulted by both the U.S. and European decision-makers regarding its feasibility.

Major X

Major X was a U.S. Air Force officer, stationed with an F-111 deployment at RAF Mildenhall, a base near London. Maj. X was uninterested in the program but turned out to be a key man in the success of the Hush House contract. Lacking personal interest, he enlisted me to write his final report on a definitive inspection trip we made to Sweden, along with another U.S. Air Force official. Needless to say, the Swedish Hush Houses were well reported and highly recommended for acquisition by the U.S. Air Force.

From long airplane conversations with Maj. X, it appeared he had been passed over for promotion to Lt. Colonel and would be invited to retire in two years. He was obviously just putting in his time.

Wing Commander Calloway

W/C Calloway was the commanding officer of Royal Air Force Base Coningsby. While he relied heavily on the decisions of Sergeant Chesters regarding the Hush House, his cooperation was essential to the revamping and provisioning of idle base facilities to house about 100 U.S. Air Force support personnel. Somehow, he also provided nearly a week's food for this contingent in the base Enlisted Men's Mess Hall. Funds for these accommodations were never mentioned. Although Calloway toiled in the shadows, he was key to the success of the test program. Any problem we encountered, he solved.

Terry Cooper

Terry Cooper was the operating head of Stainless Metalcraft, our British subcontractor, who did all the tear-down, modification and reconstruction of the Coningsby facility. Somehow, he kept his crew working during a nearly complete general strike of British labor, which reared its ugly head after we had assembled forces from three countries to conduct the USAF tests with U.S. aircraft. Terry skillfully met a difficult schedule, despite serious obstacles.

The Crew

It would be a serious error not to mention the group of employees from Stainless Metalcraft and their contribution to the Hush House test program. Despite the almost complete nationwide labor strike, these men worked 18 hour days, and more when required, to fit the Hush House test program into an elaborate and inflexible schedule involving personnel from four countries. I never found out what

Cooper did to gain their cooperation in the face of union pressure. Whatever the incentive, this crew contributed to our success beyond measure. One of them, unfortunately unidentified, saved the program singlehandedly in the dark of a weekend night.

Terry's Crew

3

Aero Systems Engineering: Rebuilding In Process

Sometimes you must call a bluff, but identifying a bluffer can be difficult and risky.

*   *   *

While seeking to expand my consulting practice into areas of more personal interest, I discovered a small, aeronautically-oriented firm in St. Paul, Minnesota. It was internationally recognized as a quality builder of jet engine thrust stands and test cells. As an adjunct to these major structures, Aero Systems Engineering (ASE) was also developing computerized data acquisition systems. With my numerous contacts in NATO countries, jet engine control experience and knowledge of computers, I presented myself to Lars Broberg, the President of ASE. I sought consideration for a job in multiple roles: international marketing and writing computer programs related to the acquisition and processing of data, from jet engines under evaluation in their test cells. I proposed a contractual relationship that involved a fixed retainer for approximately half my time and a percentage commission for products I either developed or sold. My proposal was enthusiastically received, and we began negotiating a formal employment agreement. Simultaneously, I began extensive travel and technical presentations to the U.S. Air Force at Wright Field. Working without a contract, Lars and I traded contractual papers for legal review for nearly two months when a major snag developed.

Lars Broberg, a good, practical engineer, struggled with the business aspects of running his enterprise. A Swedish firm, Granges-Nyby, had recently acquired ASE as compensation for non-payment of bills, and Lars bridled under the big-corporate yoke, which stifled his entrepreneurial style.

Granges was a very large firm, a sort of Swedish, but smaller, General Electric, with broad interests. ASE, more or less a nuisance to Grenges, was placed under the care of one of its executives, who was appointed as Chairman of the ASE Board of Directors. I met the man, Alaric Wachmeister, in the process of negotiating my employment agreement; he was a real gentleman and we got on well.

Early one afternoon, while working on a barge program at Brown Tank Corporation, I received a call from Lars Broberg.

"Alaric Wachmeister is gone and we have a new Board Chairman, Olof Muten," Lars began.

"That's an interesting turn of events, Lars, what does it mean?"

"I don't know," Lars replied, "but he'd like to meet you sometime."

"That's fine with me Lars, I'd like to meet him too."

"He's from Philadelphia, and he's here now; he would like to talk to you."

"It's pretty difficult, Lars, I'm dug-in deeply on a problem here; perhaps we could meet early this evening or have dinner together."

"He wants to see you NOW!" said Lars, with a note of real urgency in his voice. In retrospect, he sounded frightened, and I was soon to find out why. With some difficulty, I terminated what I was doing at Brown and drove to ASE some 20 miles away.

Lars nervously met me at the receptionist's desk and ushered me into a temporary office that was set up for Olof Muten. He then departed. There sat Olof, royally posed in a massive executive chair. Olof was also a Swede who emigrated to the U.S. some 25 years earlier. He was a tall, steely-eyed man who arose somewhat reluctantly to shake my hand and sat down again. I was not invited to sit and didn't. Leaning back in the reclining chair, hands clasped behind his head, he glared at me with his penetrating, blue eyes; the entire ambiance gave me the feeling I was not among friends.

"I understand we have tendered you a contract," he opened.

"That's correct, sir," I replied, quite formally.

"Are you going to sign it?" he asked.

"Everything is quite in order," I replied, "but there are a couple of small details remaining, which I'm sure we can work out." Olof smiled and leaning forward for emphasis said,

"Then you're not going to sign it, *just as it is?*"

"No," I said. "The remaining details are not a serious problem and have only to do with disposition of contingent fees, if I should slip on a banana peel." Without hesitation, Olof picked up a copy of the contract and with a flourish, gleefully tore it into many small pieces, which he deposited in the wastebasket. Then, displaying a slight smile, perhaps smirk better describes it, he said,

"Good! I don't want any f***ing consultants around my place anyway." The shot came with unrestrained savageness. I had already sized him up as a bully and responded instantly. Taking my briefcase from its resting-place on a chair, I smashed it down on the desk in front of Olof. He jumped; I think he was fearful that I was going to throw it at him. Still standing and looming over him, I moved closer and met his now wide-eyed gaze, eye to eye.

"That's fine with me Mr. Muten," I said. "Fortunately, there are enough decent people in the world so I don't have to work for a SOB like you." I didn't use the acronym. I closed my briefcase slowly, meticulously setting the clasp and without further words, turned and departed for the front door, which was about 50 feet away.

I didn't mind how it came out. If I had stayed and groveled for a job on his terms, I would forever squirm under his heel. My situation was not urgent anyway; I had enough other clients by that time to keep bread on the table. Lesson reinforced: Never have all your eggs in one basket.

As I walked toward the door, I was both inwardly disturbed and yet somehow pleased to be relieved of the burden that this relationship would have carried. I wanted to return to Brown Tank to take up the problem of the day, which the SOB had interrupted. Midway to the door, I felt an arm around my shoulder. It was Olof, walking with me. I pretended not to notice and continued toward the exit.

"Mr. Reilly, why don't you come back to my office, so we can talk? Maybe I want to keep you around here." I ignored him and kept walking. When we arrived at the door, Olof reached ahead and prevented me from opening the door. Pleadingly he said,

"Please come back to my office. Let's talk." Back in his office there was no talk, other than about my contract that we changed immediately, on my terms and signed. Thus began one of the finest, most trusted working relationships I ever had.

Olof and the Hush Houses

As our conversation turned to other topics, Olof made it clear that he viewed ASE with some disdain, which was not unwarranted. Without the acquisition by Granges, bankruptcy loomed. Its stock was severely depressed, and, as an entity in itself, it was in a state of negative net worth. Olof reoriented the conversation:

"A couple of weeks ago, I got this phone call from my old friend, Ole Lund (the president of Granges-Nyby). He said,

'Olof, I've acquired this f***ed-up little company in St. Paul, Minnesota. Could you fly out there and see what it is and what you can do with it?' So here I am. Do you have any ideas as to what we might do to put this place on the map?" Based on the conversational flow, the words carried some indication he wanted bragging rights with his old friend, Ole Lund and perhaps those other captains of industry back in Sweden. He wanted to do something BIG.

*   *   *

In the month or two I had been working with ASE, I learned that the Swedish parent company, Granges, constructed several jet engine/aircraft test cells for the Swedish Air Force and one for the British Royal Air Force. These test cells, termed 'Hush Houses,' were out of the ordinary at the time. Instead of clamping exhaust mufflers around the tail of an aircraft, they consisted of an acoustical hangar that enclosed the entire airplane. Further, the Swedish system used no water to prevent the meltdown of the muffler tube

The aircraft under test became the primary nozzle in an ejector-type pumping system, and the engine was used to induce the flow of large quantities of outside air to cool the exhaust stream. From my early experience with exhaust gas cooling at the Rosemount Labs of the University of Minnesota, I completely understood the technology and began to spin a major program for Olof.

The Hush Houses Granges built for the Swedish Air Force had not received much industry publicity at the time and were virtually unknown in the U.S.. The air-cooling technique solved many peripheral problems, and the timing was exactly correct from several different perspectives.

Environmentally, air pollution was a serious public concern.

Spraying water into the exhaust efflux of a jet engine quenched the combustion in the trailing jet and created a voluminous plume of dark, black smoke as unburned fuel burned poorly in the muffler tube. The effect was particularly bad in the afterburning mode that expelled a substantial amount of unburned fuel from the engine. Further, the unburned fuel contained residual sulfur that mixed with the cooling water and produced sulfuric acid. The resulting fine, acidic mist fell on cars and vegetation and resulted in lawsuits for damages, despite attempts to place the facilities in remote locations. The lawsuits became a nuisance to the Air Force. A frosting on the cake emerged when the U.S. Air Forces deployed in England, were forced to stand-down for an entire summer by a lack of water. Water shortages created domestic problems that forced termination of nearly all engine testing, but more of that later in the story.

From an operations and maintenance standpoint, the timing was also fortuitous. The McDonnell-Douglas F-15, was in flight test and soon to be deployed. The General Dynamics F-16 was close behind in development, as was the Northrop F-17, which with some modifications, political infighting and more engine thrust, became the McDonnell-Douglas F-18. Exhaust silencers would have to be developed specifically for each of these airplanes, because the tight-fitting cruciform structures to enclose the tail surfaces and aft fuselages of the different airplanes were necessarily of different shapes.

Operationally, the shape-fitted structure to enclose the tail of the airplane required precise, time consuming positioning of the airplane. Occasionally, damage resulted when the task was rushed or not properly performed. So, the environmental considerations, the upcoming development costs for new aircraft test cells and the operational benefits, all made the acoustical hangar an obvious choice for the future.

An added benefit for the dry, air-cooled system, was the elimination of the sulfuric acid that attacked the mild-steel structures of the water-cooled noise suppressors themselves. The water-cooled mufflers, with all their other limitations, required overhaul every two or three years. Because of the corrosion, they never lasted their contractually guaranteed, six-year, life.

The stainless steel construction of the Hush House hot sections minimized maintenance. The final clincher: When an aircraft is moved to a different base, the custom-fitted exhaust mufflers had to be relocated, along with all the associated logistics, whereas the Hush House fitted all aircraft in the inventory, up to its maximum size capacity. It was a 'perfect storm' set-up for the Hush House. However, as is often the case, logic stands aside while bureaucracy and politics rule. It would take a long journey over a tedious trail to bring success within reach.

*   *   *

Olof's steely-blue eyes danced as I spun this scenario for him; then he asked,

"What are our chances of selling Hush Houses to the U.S. Air Force?" Now it was time for the cold shower:

"Very small," I replied, "perhaps as small as half of one percent. We will be trying to change the entire Air Force testing methodology and bucking entrenched Air Force functions. Many jobs will be eliminated or reassigned with adoption of the Hush House testing concept. We will face many tough battles."

Olof loved it. He walked to a window, paused in momentary contemplation, then turned and without equivocation said, "Let's give it a try." With that, we were off and running, and Olof never looked back. Later, he would brag how he decided to go forward, even though Dick Reilly told him the chances of success were less than two percent. He moved the numeral two from below to above the line (2 vs 1/2), probably to not appear foolhardy. However, neither of us understood we were embarking on a four-year saga, and that Olof would never see the end of the ensuing complex game, to which he had committed his reputation ... and perhaps to the company's very survival.

Throughout the next 39 months Olof never wavered. In the final days, he solved the ultimate financial problem imposed by the Air Force purchasing organization in an attempt to scuttle a hard-won contract.

4

The Enemy

*When you threaten a person's career and livelihood, you
have found a true enemy.*

*   *   *

My initial explorations determined that all jet engine test
cells were procured through an office at Wright-Patterson Air Force Base (WPAFB), near Dayton, Ohio. Beginning with telephone contacts, I found the responsible people at
WPAFB and secured an appointment for a discussion of the Hush
House concept. I put together a short presentation and set out for

Dayton. There, I found a group of about 20 engineering people responsible for design and purchasing of test cells and related equipment for testing aircraft and engines. Little did I know I had met 'the enemy' on my first contact. Had I known I was entering a 39 month 'process,' I might never have started down this road.

The Rain Dance

The immediate response to our introductory presentation was somewhat strange and difficult to evaluate. The Wright Field engineering group expressed definite interest, perhaps more oriented toward curiosity than possible benefits. Initially, I didn't appreciate the size of the engineering group involved, nor the reluctance of Air Force management to interfere with established testing protocols. In addition, it ultimately developed that there was a tight little circle composed of the Wright Patterson group, two suppliers of water-cooled test facilities and an independent company dedicated to the overhaul and rebuilding of the existing test cells. Further, the major stock holder of the latter, was an ex-United States Senator with deep connections in the Washington political infrastructure. So my earliest contact with the operational organization was less than enthusiastic. Nevertheless, I was advised that the group would 'look at the concept and get back to me.'

When I checked back with the Wright Field group after some weeks had passed, the response was not positive. Paraphrasing the response:

'Air cooling might work for some smaller engines, which are common in Europe, but our TF-30 engines would burn down those air-cooled facilities in minutes.' Warning refrains on the TF-30 were to be repeated to the end, for more than three years.

The data I provided on the Swedish RM-8 engines in the Viggen fighter, had either gone unnoticed or been discarded as erroneous. The RM-8 is larger than most of the U.S. Air Force engines, and within a few percent of the largest, the Pratt & Whitney TF-30, so the reply was puzzling. In an attempt to shore up my initial thrust, I collected more information on aircraft and engines, provided pictures of operations and the maintenance history of the Swedish facilities. I also included data on the British Hush House, which Granges had built for the Royal Air Force. The latter had been in use at a fighter base in the British Midlands for over 10 years. It supported a first-line fighter, the F-4 Phantom, identical to the F-4s which were then a first-line fighter in the U.S. Air Force inventory.

The response to this more extensive presentation of data was, essentially:

'We don't believe your story.'

In response, I took a two-pronged approach: engineering and political. To clarify the technical problem, I began an aerothermodynamic analysis of large ejectors. While ejectors, sometimes called eductors, are fairly common in industrial applications and in relatively small piping systems, ejectors with primary nozzles (in this case the jet engine) two to three feet in diameter are unusual. Further complicating matters, the Hush House secondary mixing tubes, where the hot stream from the engine mixes with the cooling flow, may be 10 to 15 feet across and sometimes oval. Hence, there was little empirical data to support extrapolation, and it was necessary to resort to fairly basic analytical techniques, using momentum exchange and estimation of mixing efficiency. I submitted this analysis to Wright Field, but the response to this more extensive presentation of data was again, essentially,

'We don't believe your story.'

Into the Lion's Mouth: The Washington Arena

In addition to working on the technical credibility data, I moved up the line of action into the Pentagon's Air Staff, in Washington. There I found a sympathetic ear in the person of Major Ted Capps who was at the cutting edge of dealing with the two existing suppliers of water-cooled noise suppressors.

Capps was growing weary of the game these two companies were playing. He explained that the companies seemed to be interlocked in some sort of *competitive-appearing* process of 'you take this contract, and we'll take the next one,' via some sort of gentleman's agreement. This was possible because the water-cooled test cells were purchased against a 'Federal Stock Number' (FSN), a number such as one might find describing an item in Sears Catalog.

When an Air Force Base needed a test cell it ordered one: FSN # xxxxx, which described the product exactly without further specification. The two suppliers were at liberty to charge whatever they chose for a given system, as long as the price was no greater than what they charged commercial customers. This was, of course, a sham, since there were no commercial customers. By adjusting prices in synchronized fashion, the two companies might share the business since the Air Force always chose the lower price, allowing the two companies to share the business. Although this allegedly competitive situation prevailed for many years, there was no appearance of price fixing. The companies had reason to keep one another in the business because, if either became a 'sole source,' it would invite a great deal more scrutiny of their products and pricing structure. The apparent arrangement made it *'competitive.'*

Major Capps was immediately interested in replacing the water-cooled mufflers and began looking for ways to fit a procurement for Hush Houses into the Air Force Budget. He explained the existing game to me and told me how difficult it would be to break into which arrangement, without alerting the two companies. They would likely tie a Hush House procurement in knots using legal manipulations. One of them he said, had more lawyers on staff than engineers and played the legal game expertly.

The Technical Proposal

Meanwhile, back at Wright Field, the group responsible for designing the aircraft-specific mufflers was evaluating my analytical work. Their initial evaluations judged my analysis as valid, and I was told the test cell group 'would look favorably,' on an unsolicited proposal for the Hush House. Such an 'invitation' had to be unofficial because, by definition, an unsolicited proposal is just that: unsolicited.

*　　　*　　　*

Selling something without a Federal Stock Number to a government agency, usually follows one of two routes: solicited or unsolicited proposals. They are just what the names imply. For new or unusual purchases, the agency generates a 'requirement,' described by a specification and advertises its need in the Commerce Business Daily (CBD) – a government publication that seeks to apprise suppliers of government needs and wants. Interested suppliers follow the CBD closely and submit 'solicited' proposals describing their approach to the development of the product or service. The responding proposal includes the cost for such a development, as well as the estimated cost to purchase additional copies of the resulting article should it be deemed acceptable. The latter might be assigned a Federal Stock Number to facilitate later, routine purchases.

An alternate route is the 'unsolicited' proposal, whereby a supplier, who has what he judges to be a useful idea or product, can toss this idea into the government procurement system for consideration.

*　　　*　　　*

Accordingly, having found an 'interest' in the Hush House, I developed an 'unsolicited' proposal with the aerodynamic ejector analysis as the centerpiece. This sort of proposal was not in strict accordance with the rules of the game.

The 'unsolicited' proposal I wrote contained history, the technical analysis, cost trade-offs and logistic support costs. The WPAFB group resisted the release of support costs for the existing mufflers. This forced us to resort to the 'Freedom of Information Act,' to get historical data on the systems in current use. This delayed our proposal by several months as we waited-out the bureaucratic response. The enemy wasn't making life easy.

Our proposal compared the Hush House to the existing water-cooled test cells. These elements were combined into a book about a half-inch thick and submitted to the Wright Field test cell group. We waited for their response, while continuing the Washington game. After a month or more, we got our answer: Rejected! Worse than rejected: I was presented a 'Catch 22' that played out as follows:

'Your analysis appears valid; the general concept is good. However, we buy engine test cells under a Federal Stock Number; you don't have a Federal Stock Number. We can't assign a Federal Stock Number to a new concept without putting the system through a development and testing program. We don't have the money to buy a development program and a test article. Even if we had money, you don't qualify because our development programs are for new concepts. Your Hush House is already in operation in Europe, so it couldn't qualify for a new-concept development program. There is no way for you to acquire a Federal Stock Number.'

Boom, thud, a load of bricks hit us dead-center.

I called Ted Capps who had been industriously working to assemble funding for a development program. He was disappointed but suggested several alternate paths to be pursued. In anticipation of receiving a request for money from Wright Field, Capps had begun creating a political support structure in Washington. He suggested an immediate meeting with several people, to whom he had been selling the Hush House concept internally.

A Crucial, Chance Meeting

So it was off to Washington once again. While winter doesn't often interfere with business activity in the Midwestern United States, the East Coast is a very different place in winter.

I left on an early-morning flight for a 10:00 a.m. meeting in the

Pentagon. We landed in a mild snowstorm with perhaps two inches of the stuff on the ground – nothing by Midwest standards. It was cold, about 15 above zero when I arrived; traffic was snarled and getting a taxi was hopeless. I walked about a block to the subway station and two stops later arrived in the basement of the Pentagon.

After clearing security and going upstairs, I found Ted Capps in his office, but none of the other meeting participants had arrived. After passing a bit of time in small talk, I began wandering to the offices of the intended participants, to assess the chances of a productive meeting, while wondering whether I should just take the next airplane home.

The Pentagon was a pretty quiet place that morning. I eased open the door to a secretarial area, which served a number of offices. It was empty, but as I turned to leave, I heard a voice say,

"Hey you, c'mon in. There's nobody here, and I need somebody to talk to." A three-star general extended his hand as I entered.

"I'm Bobby Bond; what can I do for you?" I explained that I was looking for the occupant of an adjacent office.

"Forget it," said Bond. "People in this town call this bad weather when they're looking for a day off. What are you doing in town?"

For an hour or more we talked about weather, airplanes and the Hush House program. It was an opportunity to get the full attention of a key, high level Air Force executive for over an hour; no phones rang, and nobody disturbed us. I gave him my entire story in detail, finishing with the 'Catch 22,' which I had been dealt on my 'solicited' unsolicited proposal. As I finished my story, General Bond said,

"The Air Force has needed something like this for a long time, and now is the right time to do it. USAF operations in England were almost entirely shut down this past summer because of a shortage of water. Engine testing nearly ceased. Give me a copy of your proposal. I'll see that it gets to the right places and push for a proper consideration. Meanwhile, you must contact Senior Master Sergeants Mike Graham and Billy Nettles; they're the two most influential guys in the

Air Force when it comes to test cells. Graham is stationed at Headquarters, U.S. Air Forces Europe in Ramstein, and Nettles is with the Tactical Air Command at Langley Field, in Virginia. Nobody is going to buy anything like this, unless Nettles and Graham are convinced it's the right thing to do."

I returned to Major Capps' office to get a copy of the proposal from my briefcase. I told Ted what had transpired.

"That's a lucky break," he said. "You live right."

The meeting that brought me into the Washington 'snow storm' that day, never happened. I caught the afternoon airplane home, but General Bond made things happen. He was yet another stranger who crossed my path at a critical time, a key to the future. I never saw General Bond again; he was killed shortly afterward in the crash of what was likely a captured Russian fighter plane.

Our meeting was fortuitously timely.

5

London Calling

Traveling in a wilderness on a horse without a name.

*   *   *

What General Bond did internally I'll never know, but within a week or two, I received a call from the Wright Field Noise Suppressor Group. They had decided they wanted to play. They were willing to entertain a test of the Hush House concept, if Aero Systems built the facility on speculation. However, no funding was available to support such a test. I speculated this was an attempt to pacify General Bond, knowing ASE would not have the capital to invest perhaps a million dollars or more, with no assurance of follow-on business, even if the tests were successful. Nevertheless, the door had opened a tiny crack.

An Unconventional Path to a Hush House Test

I caucused with Olof. He was willing to spend a small amount of money on a test, perhaps $50,000 but no more. I suspected this was his own money. He thought the Swedes would cooperate by making one of their facilities available. However, Sweden was not a partner in NATO. I thought it unlikely the U.S. Air Force would undertake the political manipulations required to get their aircraft admitted to a country outside the usual Western/NATO diplomatic circle. I checked with Major Capps: he agreed. However, I couldn't forget the lone Hush House outside Sweden, the one the Swedes had built in England. I began to hatch a plan.

Some photographs received from Sweden, to support our proposal submissions, showed interior and exterior views of the Hush House built at the Royal Air Force Base at Coningsby, about 150 miles north of London. It was used by the RAF Strike Command, which flew McDonnell-Douglas F-4 Phantoms. These aircraft, unfortunately, had their engines mounted at about a seven-degree downward angle. To prevent the afterburner flames from impinging directly on the floor and walls of the silence tube, seven-degree ramps were added to the Coningsby facility. Aircraft to be tested were pushed backward up the ramps that leveled the engines to send their blast down the axis of the muffler tube. Because of this internal fitment, testing other airplanes at this facility would not be a simple matter of backing the airplanes in and firing off the engines.

Stainless Metalcraft, located in Chatteris, England, assembled the Coningsby Hush House. ASE had used Stainless Metalcraft for some of its test cell work, and through its owner, Cyril Cooper, I made direct contact with the Hush House at RAF Coningsby without going through a long chain of political contacts. The phone was answered immediately by Sergeant James Chesters who 'owned' the Hush House. I explained our need to look at a working Hush House and, without even asking, I received an invitation to visit.

Taking into account the admonition of General Bond – nothing will happen unless it has the approval of Sr. Master Sergeants Graham and Nettles – I contacted Sgt. Mike Graham at U.S. Air Force Headquarters, Europe (USAFE) in Ramstein, Germany (then West Germany). With some internal political difficulty, he was able to arrange military air transportation to RAF Mildenhall, near London. I flew off to London, drove to Mildenhall and waited most of a day for Graham to arrive. His airplane mechanical problems were ultimately resolved, but we reached the Coningsby Hush House a day late. Despite our delay, Sgt. Chesters welcomed us enthusiastically.

I explained my mission to Chesters, the politics of U.S. Department of Defense procurement and the need for a test of USAF aircraft, which had been imposed as a requirement. He was astute in the extreme, and I was never allowed to finish

Royal Air Force Base, Coningsby

my story as Chesters took it away from me.

"Let's do the testing here," he volunteered. This was the first and perhaps the most important step: The man whose world would be most disrupted by an outside test program was on-board instantly; only the politics, both UK and U.S., remained to be dealt with.

But a Snag Here and There

The dark side of this cordial welcome came with inspection of the test area. There were ramps and additional baffles installed in the Coningsby facility that would have to be removed to accommodate the USAF airplanes. Also, the ramps installed specifically for the F-4 Phantoms raised the thrust line of the engines, and the muffler tube was elevated to get the correct geometry. As a result, once the F-4-specific structures were removed, we would have to build and install a 'riser' to simulate a universal facility with a simple, drive-in, flat floor. Chesters suggested we talk this over with the base commander, Wing Commander Calloway.

We finished the day by meeting with W/C Calloway. Briefly, I explained the Hush House problem with the U.S. Air Force and the requirement for a test with USAF aircraft. The RAF apparently respects its top enlisted officers with the same regard the USAF attributes to its Senior Master Sergeants. Calloway turned to Sgt. Chesters and said,

"Sergeant, what will this do to your work schedule?" Chesters, who could have spiked the whole program at this point, replied,

"We can adjust our schedule to open up a week so. That would allow the Yanks time to do their thing." Then Calloway went on to say that as long as Chesters agreed, the next step was to take the question to Strike Command in London. He went on to educate us on the politics involved, saying a request to Strike should come from an equivalent level in the U.S. Air Force:

"Levels speak to equals, you know."

Back in the U.S., Maj. Capps was applying force on the Sound Suppressor Group at Wright Field. They had now been directed to work with the San Antonio Air Logistics Center (SAALC) to 'find some money' to support a test program. So the political string now extended from Dayton, Ohio to San Antonio, Texas, to the Air Staff in Washington, to U.S. Air Force Headquarters Europe in Ramstein, West Germany, to Strike Command Headquarters in London, to RAF Coningsby, with its Hush House, in the British Midlands. Getting all these entities singing from the same hymnal was going to be a challenge.

Progress was progress, but life was getting more complex at every turn. There was neither road map nor name for the process that was unfolding; just arise every morning and follow the winds of the day.

After the meeting with Calloway, Sgt. Graham and I immediately drove to Chatteris and Stainless Metalcraft, where we spoke with Terry Cooper and encouraged him to get to Coningsby and estimate the cost of removing the special features from the Hush House. I promised him drawings of the modifications that must be installed to accommodate the USAF tests. He was the de facto contractor from the outset, having built the facility some years earlier.

Graham was tasked to find the airplanes and get them assigned to the test program. I returned to the U.S. to work with Maj. Capps on arranging funding, but before that could be defined we had to hear from Graham on the specific aircraft types to be tested. These aircraft would determine the required modifications of the Coningsby Hush House. The modifications, combined with the dismantling and restoration of the Coningsby facility to its original RAF configuration, would determine the facility cost of the required tests. Graham thought he could get USAFE to cover the cost of moving the airplanes and supporting staff from Germany to England under some sort of 'training' ruse.

Ultimately it was no small deal: An F-15, an RF-4 and an F-111, plus an M-37 test stand for bare, uninstalled engines were to be accommodated. The logistics, food and housing of about 100 support people would be involved, and I wondered whether Sgt. Graham would have the political muscle to carry it off.

So, in mid 1978, we had a long, fragile chain of agreements, which would need a lot of nurturing. We were flying in the face of an old engineering axiom: 'you can't push on a rope.' Although a path to a successful test program was forming, it was evident I was riding in a wilderness on a horse without a name. On the return flight home, I contemplated the tasks ahead: It would be a long, difficult summer.

As I mentally reviewed the events of the past several months, one statement from two years prior nagged at me. It was the absolute expression of hopelessness rendered by the Wright-Patterson Noise Suppressor Group:

"You have no path to a Federal Stock Number." Was that path now emerging?

The 'no path' statement was based on the fact the WPAFB group had no money to support a test of the Hush House with U.S. Air Force aircraft. Since the path was now emerging, the program was gathering momentum and ASE was now paying for a substantial part of the test, I gambled and insisted that if the tests in England were successful, Aero Systems would be granted a Federal Stock Number for the Hush House. Unexpectedly, the Buyer in San Antonio acceded immediately. He was broadly aware of the activities in Europe, and he likely thought the testing would never happen. He produced a legally formal letter immediately, stating a Federal Stock Number would be awarded to the Hush House, upon successful completion of the Coningsby tests.

Thus, another peg fell into the proper hole and fitted wonderfully well. The existence of this document proved pivotal in the negotiation of the final contract and a major thorn in the Air Force position.

6

The Summer of '78

*It was a bit like the old stage act: The comedian frenetically
races back and forth across the stage to keep an array of
spinning plates balanced on slender sticks.*

*   *   *

Major Capps had been hard at work in my absence. I
found he had 'stolen' $35,000 from some discretionary
pot that he controlled, and it was now under the pur-
view of the San Antonio Logistics Command. Olof matched that
amount. Now, $70,000 was not a lot of money, even in 1978, so the
tests in England would have to be a frugal affair. Olof said earlier he

would go to $50,000, so I had a bit of a pad remaining if things got really tight.

I called Terry Cooper in Chatteris and inquired about his projected cost of the modification and restoration of the Hush House at Coningsby. He wanted design details, which I didn't have as yet, but Terry was a pretty accommodating guy, so we waved our hands over a trans-Atlantic telephone connection. Finally, he agreed to work on an approximate cost estimate, and I promised some more definitive design work that would enable him to sharpen his construction estimates. The floor structure was heavy but uncomplicated. The picture below shows the floor modification with Cooper doing a master's presentation of his handiwork, some months later.

Cooper Presents The Installed M-37 Thrust Stand

Designing the platform was difficult because it had to accommodate three aircraft, each having different landing gear geometry and floor support requirements with ramps to access the level but elevated, floor. The weight of the General Dynamics F-111 was nearly 100,000 pounds in the test configuration, and this weight determined the design of most of the structure. Beyond that, the problem was to set the ramp dimensions to the correct wheel tread (distance between wheels); ultimately, this turned out to be a serious problem.

*   *   *

I had been back from Europe only a few days, when in the midst of trying to gather all the design data from the Air Force, I got a frantic call from Sgt. Graham in Ramstein. He had to go to a meeting with General Bellis, the then Commanding General of U.S. Air Forces Europe (USAFE), to convince him it was a good idea to generate a 'training exercise' deploying several airplanes, support equipment and personnel, to some unfamiliar place in England. While Graham was a brilliant, hands-on, mechanical wizard, he was totally intimidated by the prospect of going before his commanding general.

"Could you help me with my presentation?" he asked.

"How can I help?" I responded

"Could you accompany me for my pitch to the general?

"When is your big meeting with the general?" I inquired.

"Tomorrow," he replied succinctly. "Could you be here?"

"It's pretty late in the day here. I'll see what I can do."

Well, that wasn't what I had planned for tomorrow, but I called Olof at his home in Pennsylvania. He was not available and there was no information on his return.

It was time for action and the plastic money again. I called for airline reservations and found I could just make an overnight flight to Germany, if I hurried. I dashed for home, packed a bag and was soon on an overnight flight to Frankfurt.

I arrived about sunrise and drove the 80 miles to Kaiserslautern, – K-town, the military calls it – near the Ramstein AFB and called Sgt. Graham. He was delighted and relieved to have some support for his meeting with the general, slated for just after lunch. Graham met me in K-town, and over breakfast, we planned his presentation. He was nervous. Military people are primarily accustomed to speaking to authority levels only one step above and one step down. Talking to 'THE GENERAL' was intimidating for him, and of course, crucial to our test program.

The big meeting turned out to be a big nothing, anticlimactic. Graham's presentation went well. Maj. Capps had likely been busy pushing the story up the command line. General Bellis had been pre-sold on the potential for air-cooling to solve his operational problems. The ghost of the water shortage from the prior summer still loomed large.

The General's command in England had been crippled by lack of rain. He repeated the story,

"The water shortage completely shut down engine and aircraft testing using the water-cooled noise suppressors." He continued, adding that he was ready for air cooling and willing to create a 'training mission' that would spring loose three first-line airplanes for testing, along with supporting staff and two C-130s to carry equipment and personnel to England. However, a new wrinkle emerged: We would have to find food and lodging for about 100 people, a significant cost I hadn't factored into the estimate. I said good-bye to a grateful, happy Mike Graham, went back to K-town, found a hotel and caught up on my sleep.

Next morning, I called Olof.

"Olof," I said, "I spent $1000 of your money last night."

"Good," he replied, "I'm sure it was necessary." Life with Olof changed since our first meeting. We discussed my options: immediate return to St. Paul or try to turn a needless trip to advantage. Some questions had already arisen regarding the modifications to the Coningsby facility, so I elected to go to Chatteris, pick up Terry Cooper, then on to Coningsby for a quick look-about and to have lunch with Sgts. Chesters and Morris. So it was an airplane to London and a drive to Chatteris, about 150 miles north.

*   *   *

The following day, Terry and I took off for Coningsby in his
father's Rolls Royce. I learned a few things from Terry and his father,
Cyril. The Roller, as the British call the Rolls Royce, is not only luxurious transportation but also a status symbol and a ticket to whatever
serves one's current whim. On one occasion, when we were lost in
London, Cyril simply stopped in heavy traffic near Lord Nelson's
monument in Trafalgar Square. We remained stationary for several
minutes, while he studied a map to determine a route to our desti-
nation. There was no honking of horns nor dirty looks. British dri-
vers, with deferential courtesy, simply parted around the Roller until
we were ready to move on. Ah, the pleasures of privilege!

Terry also introduced me to the delights of fresh cauliflower. On
the way to Coningsby at 80 miles per hour that June morning, we
screeched to a stop at a farmer's vegetable stand. Terry purchased a
giant head of cauliflower, which he replanted between the leather
seats of the Roller. We could each break off a small stalk whenever
the mood struck. Prior to that, I had never eaten cauliflower in its
raw state and never cared much for it cooked. Fresh cauliflower has
been a staple of my diet ever since.

*   *   *

At Coningsby, Sgt. Chesters welcomed us and broke out the tea
cups immediately. Chesters was refining his work schedule and had
cleared a week for our tests in September. Actually, it was better because his concept of a test week would include two weekends, a total
of nine days.

Chesters then sprang a welcome sweetener. Reaching surrepti-
tiously into his pocket, he pulled out a key and pointed to a gate in
the airport fence, made nearly invisible by overgrowing brush.

"This key fits a lock on that gate. Nobody knows I have it, or that
the gate even exists; it's supposed to be a secure area. I've cleared my
work schedule for the Thursday and Friday prior to your official
arrival on Saturday. If you guys want to get all your stuff positioned

on the road outside the gate, on Wednesday night, I'll let you in first thing Thursday morning." The extra days were a welcome relief; the timely dismantling and restoration of the Coningsby facility would present a real schedule challenge for Terry's crew.

However, the impromptu time extension would eventually prove to be a serious embarrassment for both Chesters and me. Unbeknownst to us, W/C Calloway was planning an official welcome for 'the Americans,' a major effort that included a welcoming speech and a short concert by the base's marching band.

Then I brought up the matter of billeting for the USAF flight crews and supporting staff. I inquired about hotel accommodations in the Coningsby area. I expected this to be a difficult problem, as Coningsby is a small rural village. Chesters confirmed this would be a major problem but suggested we talk to W/C Calloway again. As we were departing, we stopped-by Calloway's office. After presenting the lodging problem, Calloway responded,

"I think we can accommodate most of the crews in the enlisted men's and bachelor officers' quarters. If not, we can activate some barracks and set up beds for everyone. We will provide rations in the Enlisted Men's and Officers' Mess." It was an un-expected, gracious offer and a great relief for me, since the funds for the construction work were already stretched to the limit.

Then Calloway, put a condition on his offer.

"All I ask is that the F-15 the USAF is testing, be one of the two-seat training aircraft, and I get to fly it," – The McDonnell-Douglas F-15 was the highest performing fighter in the Western World at the time. So here was another rabbit I had to pull from an empty hat. However, General Bellis at Ramstein, had been so enthusiastic about the Hush House program, I thought I had a good chance at making good on the quid pro quo.

Terry and I returned to Chatteris in good spirits, eating 'cullies,' as he termed it, all the way. I went on to London and an overnight airplane to Minneapolis.

*   *   *

Back home, I continued the design work on the floor structure and the anchoring facilities to keep the airplanes from moving, under the high thrust of afterburner operation. I had nearly all the data on the airplanes, except for the wheel tread dimension of the F-15, which was promised imminently by the Strategic Air Command at Langley Air Force Base. As I provided each new detail, Cooper was cutting metal in Chatteris because the schedule was tight.

The F-15 landing gear dimension was getting to be more and more of a problem. Even with billions of dollars spent on the development of the F-15, the Air Force couldn't find an official drawing of the airplane that defined the essential dimensions of the landing gear. Finally, it was crunch time: Cooper needed the F-15's dimensions, or we would never meet the testing window allotted to us at Coningsby.

After another round of the Air Force facilities seeking possible sources of information, Sgt. Nettles, at TAC Langley, turned up a Colonel at the other side of the country, who was responsible for the maintenance of the lone operational F-15 squadron, located at Nellis Air Force Base near Las Vegas. I called the Colonel, explained my problem and asked if he would make two measurements of the F-15's landing gear for me. He declined, but said I could make my own measurements. Because Nellis was a secure base at the time, he made arrangements for official access and told me to bring along my passport for identity. I asked whether anyone would be available to hold the 'other end' of the measuring tape for me. He said I was on my own; the airplanes were parked on the flight line, and ordinarily, nobody was around unless flight activities were going on.

I threw a tape measure in my briefcase and commandeered a young engineering student, who was a summer intern with ASE, as a tape holder. I told him to bring his passport, and we were off for Las Vegas. During discussions on the airplane, another problem struck. Eli showed me his passport. It was an Israeli passport that wasn't going to work at a secure air force base. Although he spoke with a slight accent, I had never given his citizenship much thought. It was another problem I didn't need just then.

In Las Vegas, we rented a car and drove the 15 or 20 miles to Nellis Air Force Base. I had been giving the access problem a lot of thought and decided on the 'palms-up, shoulder shrug' approach: Gee, I'm sorry, I didn't think there would be a problem. That usually works on a one-time basis.

At the Nellis guard gate, the duty officer directed me to a nearby parking area. I told Eli to stay in the car and make himself inconspicuous. Back at the gate, I submitted my passport for inspection and found the Colonel had made the proper arrangements for me to get on the base. With a badge for me and a sticker for the car, we were off to seek the Colonel. I told Eli to stay in the car again, while I went to the Colonel's office, wondering all the while how I would handle the introduction to Eli, but luck was with me. I found the Colonel cool but cordial and totally uninterested in my problems. A lucky break; no further introductions were needed. He pointed the way to the flight line, and we were off. We made the two needed measurements, caught the late afternoon airplane for Minneapolis and were home for a late dinner.

I don't know what would have happened to me if I had been caught bringing an alien onto a secure military facility. Likely, I'd still be wearing an orange coverall, but all turned out well. Eli sent the F-15 measurements to Terry Cooper and set about completing the drawings of the support structure.

Meanwhile, the contacts we made with W/C Calloway, at RAF Coningsby and General Bellis in Ramstein, resulted in an official request to the Commanding Officer of RAF Strike Command to use the Hush House for our tests. Tentatively, all was approved, and the Coningsby Hush House would be bailed to the U.S. Air Force for nine days.

The Commander of Strike Command wanted to meet the person

who would be responsible for the testing operation and to be assured the facility would be returned to the RAF in its original condition. So it was back across the Atlantic again, for a in-person meeting with Strike Command at Lacon House, a large, military office building in London. At the close of the meeting, I owned the Coningsby Hush House for the nine-day period beginning September 23. While U.S. Air Force Europe was officially responsible for any damage that might result during the testing, I had to sign a paper saying the facility would be returned in good repair.

On my return trip, I stopped in Washington to see Major Capps. I found he was already looking forward to a successful test. He was going through procedures to cancel the contracts of the two major competitors. This was so-called 'out-year' money, the funds that had been tentatively allocated for the continuous repair and replacement of the water-cooled noise suppressors. It was an encouraging sign. Despite all the far-flung people and organizations involved, it was the first real glimmer something concrete might come of all this.

Real Trouble

On September 15, I flew back to England and drove to Chatteris to assess progress at Stainless Metalcraft. The general work-plan was to fabricate sub-assemblies in Cooper's shop and truck them to Coningsby, where they would finally be assembled. This would minimize the time required to work on the facility and leave the most time for the aircraft and engine testing.

On arrival at Stainless, the outlook was bleak. Work had stopped on fabricating the necessary components for raising the floor of the Coningsby facility. On a Friday night, with only a week to go, Stainless Metalcraft was on strike; almost the entire country was on strike. While this was the time of Margaret Thatcher, she hadn't yet completed working her magic. British labor unions virtually ran the country. Terry Cooper was concerned but not despondent. Not to worry he said, but I could see he was troubled. There was nothing I could do, so I found a hotel to recover from the jet lag. Back at Cooper's factory in the early morning, I found two people working. I didn't know what Terry did to achieve this miracle, but it was a welcome sign. By noon, approximately 20% of the welding was completed and by nightfall, almost half the welding was done. There was hope. After Mass on Sunday, I drove to a glider port at Lasham, where I had made some friends years earlier. I managed to get in a couple of flights, which put the thought of welding steel temporarily out of mind.

Slingsby Capstan

After the Darkness the Dawn

Back in Chatteris Monday morning, I found Cooper's crew had worked over the weekend, and the fabrication was nearly complete. Cooper and I took off in 'the Roller,' driving about the British countryside, arranging for rental of a crane and attending to other details for the coming week.

On Tuesday, we dropped south toward London to visit U.S. Air Force personnel operating from a RAF base at Mildenhall. The Mildenhall group was providing the F-111 for the test, and we wanted to get the tie-down cabling so we could match the fittings for the tests at Coningsby.

We went over the test schedule and confirmed the F-111 would arrive on the proper day. The crew chief for the F-111 looked at our schedule and test plan and shook his head.

"That's a pretty ambitious schedule; I hope you know what you're doing," he said, skeptically. Later he drew me aside, out of Cooper's hearing range and said quietly,

"You'll never do it with blokes." (British slang for the working man). He continued, "They arrive late in the morning, then it's tea at 10:00, a long lunch hour, afternoon tea and early quitting-time."

This mood prevailed even after the entire USAF cadre and airplanes arrived at Coningsby. Serious money began to be wagered among the U.S. crews. Bets were placed on whether we would test even one airplane during our allotted week. The Americans stationed at Mildenhall had much experience with British contractors working at their base, and in those years British labor controlled the empire.

Finishing the day back at Coningsby, a last-minute talk with Chesters confirmed his key to the hidden gate worked properly, and he was in the clear for accommodating us on Thursday morning, as promised. We finished our day in Calloway's office to arrange for billeting of Cooper's men, who would be accommodated in the enlisted men's quarters on the base. It was a lucky break that the RAF was providing not only sleeping quarters but also food in the enlisted men's mess. Calloway never disclosed how he funded this 'boarding house.' After what Cooper had been through, he needed this stroke of good fortune. I don't know either, what incentives Cooper gave his men to work through the national labor strike, but it was likely expensive.

We spent Wednesday getting all the remaining details together, so we were ready to roll early Thursday morning. I lay awake much of the night, wondering whether all the pieces would fit together, but one way or another, we were standing in the gallows hoping the trap door would hold.

7

The Eleven-Day Week

Somehow Cooper brought it all together. I never learned how he got his crew to ignore union orders or whether retributions of some sort were visited on them by their union, but they got the job done.

* * *

Before sunrise on Thursday, we moved out of Chatteris with three truckloads of structural components and tools, a mobile crane and some auxiliary vehicles. We arranged this convoy on the airport perimeter road, as instructed by Sgt. Chesters, and waited for him to appear. We were not officially 'on base,' so we couldn't announce our arrival. Chesters appeared momentarily, and the great adventure began.

Chesters unlocked the gate. We chopped away the underbrush that concealed its location, and the trucks rolled in at 10:50. The 'blokes' went to work with a real vengeance. By 11:30 they had the

ramps loose and one of them removed by 1:40. After a 20-minute lunch, the crew was back, working like quarry slaves. By 3:00 both ramps were out and stored for replacement when the tests were completed. Then we hit a

Original Configuration

speed bump: The large, interior, acoustic baffles were welded into place during erection of the building, and now the welds holding them were hidden. After much puzzlement, one of the men hit upon a solution, which involved blind cutting with reciprocating saws, but it was tedious work. Despite a lot of invisible accomplishments, little further progress was evident when we finally quit for dinner about 7:00.

Sgt. Chesters somehow had arranged for early sleeping accommodations for Terry's crew on the base, although we hadn't officially arrived. However, he was unable to arrange for meals, so the crew piled into a couple of cars and searched the countryside for an ancient rural pub that served meals. Terry and I found a 'Blimpy' stand (a sort of British McDonald's), downed a hamburger and went back to work sawing at the cantankerous welds. Later in the evening, one of the 'blokes' appeared, to watch the proceedings, but soon, whether out of responsibility, guilt, or embarrassment, he picked up a torch and began to cut away some fastenings. The three of us flailed away until nearly midnight. Terry and I collapsed in a small hotel in Coningsby town.

Early on Friday morning, the crew was hard at work removing the baffles. It was difficult work, and it took until about 8:00 in the evening to get the entire space cleared of the RAF's special fittings. By 11:00, we had moved our internal platform and ramps inside and began preliminary alignment of the various sub-assemblies for final welding. Then, everyone crashed for the night. The workmen, while exhausted, were doing right-well.

Embarrassment

Saturday dawned a bright fall day, a lucky break because we were going to need good traction on the asphalt apron to conduct pull-testing of the tie-down anchors. The crew was at work early, completing the various weldments and fittings. This was officially to have been our first day on the base. Work was really humming along in the warm, morning sun, when an RAF staff car pulled up on the hangar apron, accompanied by a large blue bus.

Wing Commander Calloway popped out of his car and came over to me with hand extended.

"Welcome to Coningsby," he greeted. We talked briefly, and he expressed surprise at the amount of work that had been done in an hour's time. I muttered something about how efficient Terry's boys were, but my words were drowned by the first strains of "The Star-Spangled Banner." This was followed by "God Save the Queen." Calloway had organized the base marching band to appear on a weekend morning and welcome us to Coningsby.

I accompanied Calloway as he walked around, inspecting the completed work. When we walked out of sight, alongside the facility, Calloway saw the great stacks of steel components that had been removed from the interior over the past two days. He seemed surprised and remarked,

"I suspect Chesters had a hand in this; welcome to Coningsby," he repeated with a knowing smile, then turned to his car and drove off. I never learned whether Chesters encountered any trouble for turning our nine-day approval into eleven days.

Real Trouble

After the band stopped playing, Terry's blokes finished installing the new steel hardware and welding it into place. By early evening, an assembly of trucks, cranes and a fuel 'bowser' was lined up outside the hangar. The assembly was connected to the engine thrust stand anchors by an array of block and tackle, huge clevises and pins. Then an unforeseen snag developed: The attachments to the dynamometer and the block-and-tackle sheave were incompatible. A different clevis (a D-shaped fitting with a pin across the straight element of the 'D,' photo right) was required, not a good development on a Saturday night. We were dead in the water until Monday, and even then, the availability of such a massive clevis would be several hours away. While others stood around, cursing the fates and the darkness, Sgt. Morris tapped me on the shoulder.

"C'mon," he said, motioning me out into the night. "I don't want to discuss this in front of all these people." I would later find out why. Morris and I made our way several hundred yards across the darkened airport.

"There's a big clevis on the crash-crane, but tampering with it is a Court Martial offense. Nobody is flying on a Saturday night so it's no great risk; we'll 'nick,' it and return it in the morning. I think it's good to 100,000 pounds." It took both of us to carry the clevis. Sgt. Morris was one of those unstoppable people, who came into my life at a time of real need. He was an example of people who will go to the utmost ends, to get the job at hand completed.

The crash-crane is crucial to fighter operations. In the event of an accident, it is used to quickly clear the runway so other orbiting aircraft, which might be short of fuel, can land. Once the big clevis in the photo opposite, was installed in the load string we pulled 32,000 pounds easily, child's play.

Nobody was unkind enough to ask where he got the clevis; some people knew where it came from and others didn't. So it was on to the big pull on the anchor for the F-111: 30 metric tonnes, about 66,000 pounds.

The load requirement, as set by Base Engineering, was a surprise. In planning talks, the discussions mentioned proof-loading the restraining hardware 'to a bit more than the maximum engine thrust,' or about 30,000 pounds for

Test Load Line With Large Clevis

the TF-30 in the F-111. I had done the restraint design for 35,000 pounds, only to be blindsided by a nearly-doubled requirement.

With the stronger clevis in-hand, the load string was then re-arranged and attached to the aircraft anchor point. The winch on the block-and-tackle was engaged, and we watched as the needle on the dynamometer moved slowly upward. At slightly over 35,000 pounds, the entire string of trucks and crane began to move; we were barely over halfway to our proof load. We topped-off the first bowser with more fuel and added the last available fuel bowser into the string. That arrangement produced a bit over 50,000 pounds, still a long way to go.

Terry Cooper and I got into a fairly heated argument. He wanted to pull against the front structure of the hangar. I objected because I had no idea how the structure was secured below ground, and I was personally responsible to the RAF for damages. In my opinion, the only way out was to add weight and get more rubber on the asphalt. Cooper mentioned that 'Dennis Cranes' had a really big, heavy crane. Since construction labor was on a national strike, it was likely available. After a lot of telephoning, Terry found someone in authority with Dennis Cranes who agreed to meet him at 8:00 Sunday morning to sign the rental papers. However, there remained a major problem. The large crane was in Boston, on England's east coast, some 60 miles away. It had a maximum speed of 5 miles/hour, so at best, we were going to lose an entire day, and perhaps two, while the crane was moved from Boston on Monday.

We worked until after 10:00, cleaning up the odds 'n ends, so we could be ready for the airplanes, which were to arrive on Monday; but it was a sleepless night. What if the anchor didn't hold? A check of my design calculations looked as though we might be all right, but suppose it failed. How long might repairs and reinforcements take? The terrors of the night took over.

*　*　*

That night, I was assigned a luxurious room in the Bachelor Officers' Quarters. It came complete with my own 'batman,' a personal valet to attend to my every need. Traditionally, in the old British military, every officer was assigned a batman, and in the BOQ at Coningsby the tradition continued. An encyclopedic entry describes a batman's duties:

> * *acting as a "runner" to convey orders from the officer to subordinates*
> * *maintaining the officer's uniform and personal equipment as a valet*
> * *driving the officer's vehicle, sometimes under combat conditions*
> * *acting as the officer's bodyguard in combat*
> * *other miscellaneous tasks the officer does not have time or inclination to do*
>
> *The action of serving as a batman was referred to as "batting." In armies, where officers typically came from the upper class, it was not unusual for a former batman to follow the officer into later civilian life as a domestic servant.*

Unaccustomed to such service, I was a bit embarrassed by having my bath drawn each night and being awakened gently with a hot basin of water for shaving. I felt really sorry for my batman because we were working until nearly midnight each night and were up early in the morning. I told him to take the days of my stay there as a mini-vacation, but he was there every night, with my jigger of rum, when I arrived. I gave him my rum, which I think he appreciated, since he was always on duty regardless of my hours; I needed no soporific. It was a nice touch, in a strange way, but I never overcame the embarrassment of being waited on.

Salvation

The Pull-String

I arose early and went to Mass in Coningsby town, while Terry drove off to Dennis Cranes to arrange the paper work for crane rental. After breakfast in the officer's mess there was little else I could do, but I went to the Hush House to clean up loose ends. As I drove through our 'secret' gate, I was astounded to see a huge crane, already aligned into our pull-string and ready to be attached to the existing train of vehicles. Only one man was there. He had the big crane in position ready for the final test.

"Where did that come from?" I asked. He smiled knowingly and replied,

"I nicked it (stole it) off a job on the coast." The night before, while Terry was calling to find a representative for the traveling crane rental, one of Terry's men, who somehow knew of the crane's location, took it upon himself to solve the problem in his own way. Using his personal car, he drove to Boston, on the British east coast, and effectively 'stole' the crane. He made the 12-hour drive back to Coningsby overnight, at its top speed of five miles per hour.

Fortunately, the trip was mostly in the dark and didn't attract the attention of the highway police. I don't know how he would have handled questioning, had authorities stopped him, while he was driving a stolen crane.

Cooper arrived a few minutes later, despondent; he was not successful in contacting Dennis Cranes, another day lost. When he saw the newly acquired crane, he too was astonished but grateful.

Despite all the sweating and straining to get adequate anchoring for proof-loading the tie-downs and fixtures, the actual test was over quickly. The big crane, with its added weight and rubber on the tarmac, was the last piece of the puzzle. Without delay, we cranked on the ready tow-string, reached 66,000 lbs. on the dynamometer, took a picture of the dial as evidence and quit for the day. Our crew, who had worked 20-hour days, needed a break. We were now a day ahead of schedule, with all the high hurdles behind us.

I thanked Cooper's man profusely for his contribution to the schedule, which was potentially heading into a serious problem.

"Aw, it was nuthin'," he protested.

But it was really '*something*.' He saved the entire program from impending disaster. In the ensuing chaos, I never learned his name. He left quickly after the load test.

"Ought to get it back before they miss it," he said with a smile, as he climbed into the crane's cab and drove off on another 12-hour, 60-mile trip, to have the crane in place for Monday morning operations, should the strike be settled."

He never returned to the Hush House. Sadly, he probably didn't realize the importance of his night's work as he disappeared into the morning's mists, at five miles per hour. Cooper assured me he would 'take care of him.'

*   *   *

The Dambusters

I spent the remainder of Sunday, visiting some locations having to do with the operations of the 617 Squadron during WW II. RAF Coningsby was the home of the Squadron, known as The

Dambusters. 617 Squadron trained at Coningsby for months, to execute one of the most extraordinary air raids of the war. A British engineer, Barnes Wallis, came up with a proposal to cripple a major

segment of German industry. He designed a bomb, with a cylindrical shape, that skipped along the surface of the water behind a dam. It was launched

Lancaster Drops Wallis' Bomb

with rotation, and as its forward motion slowed to a near-stop upon reaching the dam, the rotation caused it to crawl down the inner surface of the dam.

To make all the physics come out correctly, the bomb – carried by the RAF's largest bomber, the Lancaster – needed to be dropped very precisely at night from an altitude of a few feet above the water. The exact height was determined by lights mounted at the front and rear of the Lancaster, and pointing fore and aft at precise angles. When the spots of light converged on the water's surface, the altitude was exactly correct, about 30 feet as I recall, and the bomb was re-

Mohne Dam Breached

leased. The targets were the Mohne, Eder and Sorpe Dams, major sources of electric power for German industry in the Rheur Valley. The dams also provided water for a large segment of the German civil population.

Some idea of the flying skill required, is illustrated in the recent (2008) photograph of a recreation of the 1943 raid on its 65th anniversary. It shows the only remaining Lancaster flying in Europe, passing over the Derwent Dam in England. The depiction is similar

Derwent Dam

to the Mohne, because anti-aircraft guns were stationed on the towers above the dam. By flying low on the approach and departure, the Lancasters remained below the firing angle of the German defensive guns.

The successful raids, carried out in May of 1943, required months of night practice runs on dams in the British Midlands. Crews were housed in relatively luxurious quarters at Petwood Hall, now a luxury hotel, in Wood-hall Spa, a small city near RAF Coningsby. The Lincoln Lounge at the hotel, is now a miniature museum, displaying pictures and memorabilia from those practice years. Just above the framed Lancaster in the picture, right, is a moderately large pine tree that was driven through the windshield of one of the

Miniature Museum

Lancasters during a night practice mission.

*   *   *

Back to Work: The Test Week

Finally, after all these months of people contacts, money searches and approvals, of one sort or another, it was time for the tests, the focus of it all. The test specification was relatively simple: Run the U.S. Air Force's largest and nastiest engines in the facility, measure the acoustic attenuation, and inspect the muffler tube to ascertain any resulting damage. Of course, this was all done in maximum power and in after-burning mode, to impose the maximum stress on the facility. Observers, with acoustic meters, were positioned in a 100 meter diameter circle, every 45 degrees around the exit of the muffler tube. Despite all the preparation difficulties we'd been through, the tests themselves were was somewhat anticlimactic and were finished in a few hours.

First Test Aircraft F-15

The F-15, with its Pratt & Whitney F-100 engines, was the first test aircraft. Because it was a first-line fighter, it had to be returned to Ramstein as soon as possible. Acoustically, the facility performed well and detailed examination after the test revealed no damage. As the F-15 climbed out to work back in Germany, I hoped W/C Calloway got his ride, but I was too busy to check on it.

It was time for the F-111 the USAF personnel feared 'would burn the place down.' The General Dynamics F-111 was rolled into the facility at dusk. We had some difficulties due to the size and weight of the aircraft. It fit into the RAF facility but just barely and with the wings in swept position. There was a problem with the length of a cable bridle that attached to the landing gear, and the airplane had a minor instrumentation problem.

In the center of this chaos, a needed air compressor ran out of fuel, a real problem in the middle of the night with everything locked and unavailable. Sgt. Morris, always up for the task at hand, grabbed a piece of tubing and started to siphon gasoline from a near-by Jeep, a

General Dynamics F-111

violation of RAF regulations. Just at that time, Wing Commander Calloway, who had a way of turning up at inconvenient times, arrived. He saw the offending siphon in operation, and immediately approached Sgt. Morris, who was bent over the gasoline can and unaware of Calloway's presence. All other work stopped and there was an eerie silence as Calloway stood over Morris and his siphon. Finally, Calloway quietly said,

"John, that's against regulations you know." The surprised Morris stood up, saluted smartly, and said,

"It's all right Sir, as you can see I have the container properly 'earthed' (grounded, as we would say)." Although there was no wire connecting the gasoline container to the jeep, the container was resting on the ground after all. Calloway gave him a fatherly reprimand and an admonition:

"Don't let this happen again."

The following day, Tuesday, the F-111 test went off smoothly, without difficulty, so the worst of the airplanes was now finished, and we began to relax somewhat. We had until Sunday to run the F-4, two uninstalled engines and to rework the facility.

Uninstalled Engine Tests

We swung the M-37 engine test stand into place, secured it, and installed the F-100 engine. Everything was up to the USAF personnel from then on. Things became a bit disorganized because it was the first M-37 thrust stand ever to be delivered to the European Command, and it was not used or even tested before the Coningsby tests.

Pratt and Whitney F-100

The M-37 was a real masterpiece of test equipment, totally automated. Once activated, the computer package that accompanied the mechanical system, started the engine, ran the designated tests, recorded all the data, ran the engine through a cool-down cycle and shut it down, all untouched by a human operator. The automated system proved to be a problem in our particular case because the final step in the sequence was to open a dump valve to empty the engine's fuel control system after engine shutdown.

From the pictures it is evident that given the maze of elevating structural members, three gallons of fuel dumped on the floor would create a difficult clean-up problem. The solution proposed, was to stop the automated program before this final step occurred. This was particularly critical because the last engine to be run, the TF-30 used in the F-111, required us to do a small modification to the floor structure. This involved flame cutting and welding. We couldn't tolerate any fuel contamination, which would pose a fire hazard during the modification process.

Sgt. Morris In Trouble Again

You're probably ahead of me already. The F-100 was started, run through its paces, cooled and stopped. Then, unexpectedly, the dump valve opened. The fuel sump emptied into the voids between the structural members. A long cleaning process began and ran on into the middle of the night. The entire area was flooded with water, and with mops and brooms, we attempted to encourage the water/fuel mixture to flow toward a lone floor drain.

After several hours of flushing, pushing and mopping, the odor of fuel vapor remained strong, and the use of cutting torches and welding tools was potentially dangerous. The water remaining on the floor reflected the rainbow sheen of the oil film floating on the water's surface. The welder stood-by, waiting for a decision on 'what next' when Sgt. Morris grabbed a high-pressure water hose and crouching low between the structural members, directed a stream of water aimed to hold back the shallow wall of water/oil mixture. Holding the volatile mixture at bay he shouted to the welder,

"OK, cut!" Firing his torch, the welder quickly accomplished the necessary cutting.

The welding would take a bit longer, but Morris aimed his water hose again, and the welding began. Just then, Wing Commander Calloway arrived in his staff-car. Calloway seemed to have a sixth sense that homed-in on potential trouble. He got out of his car, watched the action for a moment and walked toward the welder, who immediately extinguished his torch. Morris, concentrating on his task with his back turned to the action, was oblivious of Calloway's arrival. Calloway finally tapped Morris on the shoulder to get his attention. Morris jumped to attention and saluted the officer.

"What's going on here John?" he asked. Morris didn't reply but carefully dried his hands while searching for a credible answer. Then he took Calloway by his shoulders, turned him around gently and guided him toward his car.

"Sir," he said, "there are things going on out here that you really don't want to know about. If we somehow blow this place sky high we'll really need your help, but until then you're best-off in your office. It will save you a lot of worry." The base commander drove away, as directed by one of his enlisted men.

We finished the modification in short order and ran the TF-30 engine the following morning. That completed the required tests by noon Wednesday, and Cooper began restoring the facility to its original state. The USAF contingent departed, completely satisfied with the performance of the facility. In the celebratory moments of a successful completion of all the scheduled tests, I extracted a promise from Calloway that there would be no disciplinary action taken against Sgt. Morris.

A Little Diversion

Bob Lucas, the President of Aero Systems, and I took Thursday off and drove to Lincoln to see the fabled Lincoln Cathedral, dating to the 12th century. Completed in 1235, it is considered one of the more beautiful structures in Europe. One

Lincoln Cathedral

of four original copies of the Magna Carta has resided safely in its archives for over 800 years.

After Lincoln, we drove to Nottingham, the environs of Robin Hood and his merry men. However, England produced an entire day of pouring rain, for which the country is famous, so my memory of

Nottingham Castle

Nottingham is limited to the interior of its castle and green countryside, as viewed through a foggy windshield. We returned to Coningsby that evening and took Sergeants Chesters and Morris to dinner.

We suggested as grand a dinner as we might find in a small village. However, Chesters suggested we should visit a famous old pub in the area, the 'Blue Bell Inn,' which served traditional, old-English meals. The place dated from 13th century, a time when nutrition was haphazard, and the occupants were of smaller stature. Ceilings were about five feet 10 inches, more or less, so I had to hunker down and bend my neck a bit.

The fare was also 13th century with offerings such as 'Ploughman's Lunch,' a thick piece of cheese with coarse bread and fruit, and 'Shepherd's Pie,' a lamb, potato and vegetable dish resembling a chicken pot pie, except for the lamb. I had the Shepherd's Pie, although I'm not usually partial to lamb.

We had a great time reliving the trials and the successes of the week in

Blue Bell Inn

the ambiance of 700 years past. It was a small thanks to two people who played a very large role in the ultimate success of the Hush House program. Again, two people passed through my life and made things happen for me at a critical time.

The eleven-day week was completed in eight days. After Terry Cooper completed the restoration of the Hush House to its original state, we met with W/C Calloway to officially return custody to the RAF. All concerned were pleased, and only the final report to USAF Headquarters remained to be completed. This turned into yet another 'final' problem, as related in the following chapter.

8

Money And Politics: The Budget Of 1980

It's always the money, ... and especially the politics.

*   *   *

Returning to the U.S., I found Maj. Capps had been hard at work assembling funding for a really significant purchase of Hush Houses. Word of the successful tests at Conings-by filtered back from USAFE Headquarters Europe, and pressure was being applied to get initial units built in Europe. Capps' funding scheme was fairly complex because the new-found urgency meant the Hush House program could not be integrated into the current budget

POM Cycle. The POM (Program Objective Memorandum) that describes the purpose of the program, should be closely tied to the advance budgetary planning. The POM Cycle was typically a six-year process, far outside the objectives of General Bellis, the USAFE and Olof's urgency, of course. Getting the program funded outside the traditional budget planning process was going to be tricky but not impossible. It's done frequently and requires an intimate knowledge of the budgeting process. Some political connections are also helpful. I had neither at the time.

Unusual Opportunity

A slowing in the immediate activities, provided a singular opportunity to give the program a real push. I had only been back in the U.S. for a short time, when I got another urgent call from Sgt. Graham at USAFE, in Ramstein.

"Look," he began, "I've written my final report on Coningsby six times already, but my Colonel wants the thing written by a PhD in English, and I'm in over my head. Can you help me?" He was angling for me to make yet another quick trip to Germany, which wasn't my short term plan. Weary of the trans-Atlantic shuttle, I told him I would be glad to help him, but I needed to have a copy of his report to know what it was he wanted to say. I offered to edit it and return it quickly.

His Colonel had him on a time-line that wouldn't allow airmail, and at the time, the slow-speed teletype was the only means of hard-copy communications that would meet the required schedule. It was already Friday night in Europe, and Graham was committed to submit his report on the following Monday. We finally agreed he would telex his draft immediately, and I would return it Sunday night. I waited several hours as the Telex machine hammered out more than 20 feet of laborious text, at 10 characters per second, plus delays.

Reading the first few pages gave me an understanding of what Graham wanted to say. He was fine, worthy technician, but as his Colonel said, he didn't have a PhD in English, nor did I. I took the document home and began to rework it. Finally, taking Graham's major points as an outline, I rewrote the report in its entirety. On Sunday I went to ASE to enter it, character-by-character, into the Teletype machine. Because of the slow-speed nature of the machine, it wasn't quite like typing, and any attempt at speed overran the machine's mechanical system.

Needless to say I suppose, it was a 'postive' report. I got many a chuckle in the ensuing year, as functionaries up and down the political chain would show me 'the official report' or the 'government's official position' on the Hush House.

A Plunge Into the Budget

The government's current-year budget contains items slated for immediate funding, but it may also look forward to needs in following years. The water-cooled noise suppressors, for example, might be budgeted for acquiring a few totally new units the current year, but the plan would also require money for the known need to overhaul and maintain the entire inventory of noise suppressors in future years. These funds are known as 'committed but not obligated,' and in the fertile mind of Maj. Capps, contained the essence of a Hush House budget.

Federal funds often have different 'colors,' in this case 'one-year money' (the currently funded programs) and 'three-year money,' which is committed to be spent but not obligated to be spent just yet, also termed 'out-year money.' With the success of the Hush House tests and the projected replacement of the water-cooled suppressors, the so-called 'out year' money, for their repair and maintenance, would not be required. Capps simply canceled the contracts of the competitors, freeing the extended funding that had not yet been 'obligated.' He then had a reasonably good start for buying a Hush House program, with the number of facilities not yet specified. Capps and I informally planned for about 25 facilities, at $1.5 million each, which rounded up to about $39 million, but we never spoke aloud about the number. It was closely held between us.

The 'Spinning Plates'

I was soon making several trips each month to San Antonio for discussions with San Antonio Air Logistics Center, the ultimate contracting agency. Engineering, Contracting and Field Operations people all had to be satisfied it was safe to abandon the water-cooled test facilities. This was a slow, arduous process, and I struggled to keep things moving on the technical front to match the rapidly developing happenings in Europe and Washington. The Project Engineer, a reliable and well-respected 'Old Timer,' was cautious. However, after returning from lunch one day, while chatting in his office, he leaned back in his chair, stared vacantly at a spot on the ceiling and mused aloud.

"You know, this is *really* a better way to test aircraft and engines, but we have to find a way to get [a competitor's] Congressman off our back." I couldn't wait to get home and look up just who was the competitor's Congressman; it was Dan Flood who was in deep ethical trouble in the House of Representatives.

A news clipping from the day read:

> *The Honorable Daniel Flood, flamboyant subcommittee chairman of the House Appropriations Committee, was indicted by a federal grand jury in Los Angeles in 1978 on charges of lying about payoffs he allegedly received.*
> *Flood, then 74, was charged with lying to a grand jury in June 1977 when he denied receiving $5,000 in cash from a departed trade school operator and denied taking $1,000 in cash from a former Washington lobbyist. This was part of a kickback scheme involving a chain of west-coast trade schools.*
> *Flood's top aide, Stephen B. Elko, was convicted of bribery and started cooperating with the feds. He told them that Flood took in more than $100,000 in bribes in return for political favors.*

The then-current "Time Magazine" said,

> *"Dapper Dan, as he was known, sports a villainous-looking, waxed mustache and favors wildly eccentric clothes — velveteen suits, ruffled shirts, patent-leather*

shoes and satin-lined capes. But despite his outlandish
appearance, Dapper Dan Flood, 74, amassed immense
power in his 30 years on Capitol Hill."

Ultimately, he was censured for bribery and forced to resign his
seat in the House of Representatives, thus removing a major roadblock to the Hush House contract.

Exactly what was going on in the background could only be a
matter of conjecture rolled up in the phrase, 'Getting [a competitor's] congressman off our back.' In this and many other ways, I
was blessed with good fortune throughout the development of the
program; I never had to do battle with Dan Flood in Washington.

The Budget Fight

In Washington, Capps' 'theft' of the out-year money yielded about
$15 million, as I recall, leaving us about $24 million short of our 'pie
in the sky' projection for 25 facilities. This meant we somehow had
to get the program into the 1979 budget bill (to be enacted in 1980),
then taking shape in Congress. This meant entirely bypassing the
Authorization Process (see Appendix A for a detailed description of
how the Final Budget Bill is passed). The trick in this sort of manipulation is to get your program entered into both the House of Representatives and Senate budget bills as 'line items' (an item that has its
own numbered, specific line in the federal budget), a daunting task
for an outsider.

I went to my district Congressman, Bruce Vento, for help. Vento's history revealed him as having a big ear for labor unions but not
being very active in the defense business. Yet again, another Good
Samaritan entered the picture.

Vento's Legislative Assistant, welcomed me warmly. An immi-
grated, ex-British citizen, he a PhD in Political Science and had been
active in U.S. politics for a number of years. He directed Walter
Mondale's Vice Presidential campaign at the state level. As a reward
for his service, when Mondale became Vice President under Carter,

he became the liaison officer between the Central Intelligence Agency and the Vice President's office and knew well the entire political community. Later, while with the National Security Agency, one of his duties was to disassemble highly classified programs (so called 'black programs'), into unrecognizable pieces and bury them in the budgets of Agriculture, Health & Welfare, Education and other innocuous places. With pieces small enough and renamed, they became unidentifiable – yes, our enemies read the finished budget carefully, looking for evidence of 'black' program expenditures. When the budget bill was passed, he would then collect his 'plants' and see that the funds were assigned to their intended destinations. He was the absolutely perfect tool for my job. He had complete access to most of the details of the federal budget. When I explained my problems to him he responded,

"Not a problem, I have friend over in Drafting. Currently, they're drafting the 1980 budget bills. I'll give him the right words and he'll see they get in both the House and Senate bills. Consider it done."

When the Hush House funding appeared in the 1980 Budget – in guarded words, of course – many were surprised at the 'windfall,' but only three people knew how it got there.

9

Boondoggle?

Everyone likes a little sightseeing travel.
Yet another diversion.

*   *   *

Within a month of my return from the Coningsby tests, I was in San Antonio for discussions with the procuring agency, the Air Logistics Center, when a new face appeared in the San Antonio mix. Mr. Z, who had been an apparently casual observer at the Coningsby tests, suddenly appeared to have a more influential role. He was Chief of the Intermediate Maintenance

Branch of NORAD (North American Air Defense Command), the last-ditch defense command center, housed deep underground in the Rocky Mountains, near Colorado Springs. NORAD's interest and leverage in aircraft and engine testing was never explained. Sgt. Graham's report apparently trickled around the system and triggered NORAD's interest. Mr Z's song was, to paraphrase,

'Yes, the Hush House appears to be wonderful, but we've only seen one facility. We are putting all our eggs in one basket, by going with the Hush House, Air Force wide. Let's see some more of them. We should get some view of long-term reliability and maintenance and should see some older facilities.'

Even though the RAF Coningsby facility had been supporting Strike Command's F-4s for over five years, without indications of significant maintenance, Mr. Z wanted more evidence of really long-term durability. I pointed out that the Swedes had been using the air cooling technique, for over a decade, with excellent life cycle costs. The response was:

"Let's go and look at some of their facilities."

Apparently, Mr. Z was positioned to stop the show, and it was clear that the budget manipulations going on in Washington might be going nowhere without Mr. Z being satisfied. In short order, a cadre of visitors was cooked up, and I had Olof arrange an itinerary to visit four of the Swedish facilities. USAFE was pressing for a Hush House contract by the first quarter of 1980, so the trip had to be quickly executed. Visas and military travel orders for the participants would take a month, minimum, so the trip was set for early December.

Initially, the traveling entourage was to include Maj. Capps from the Pentagon Air Staff, Ed Sherwood, the San Antonio ALC Project Engineer, Mr. Z and Major X, from the USAF contingent at RAF Mildenhall. Ultimately, scheduling conflicts reduced the group to two, Mr. Z and Major X, and we agreed to meet in London in early December, with follow-on travel to Sweden.

Arriving at London Heathrow, I found Mr. Z's flight was canceled, further complicating an already tight schedule. I called Maj. X at Mildenhall and found he hadn't yet left to meet me at Heathrow, a lucky break. I explained the situation to him, and since he had access to the Air Force's electronic grapevine, I suggested he try to find out what happened to Mr. Z. I contacted Gosta Agmen, the Granges-Nyby engineer who was hosting the group in Sweden. I asked him to push everything forward one day, found a hotel near the airport and got some sleep.

Waking late in the day, I called Major X who found Mr. Z was due in on the same flight as originally planned but one day later. The day's delay drove a decision to reverse the order of the planned visits in Sweden, starting from Malmo in the south and ending in Stockholm.

Still, Another Snag

I was at the airport at dawn, met Mr. Z's flight, found Maj. X, and mid-morning, we boarded a flight to Copenhagen. En route, I explained the visit's order-reversal, and that we were meeting Gosta Agmen at the airport in Copenhagen. He would guide us through Copenhagen to the ferry terminal. Malmo, Sweden was a short two-hour boat trip across the Oresund, the narrow strait connecting the Baltic and North Seas. It was only at this point that Maj. X waved a red flag.

The start from Malmo, required about a ten-mile trip on Danish soil from the airport to the ferry terminal. His military orders did not cover travel in Denmark. The airport complied with Major X's orders, essentially an international no-man's-land, but he was not authorized to set foot in Denmark proper. Mr. Z, being a civilian Air Force employee, 'thought he was OK' to enter Denmark.

Neither Major X nor Mr. Z appeared to be experienced travelers. They were not accustomed to rolling with uncertainties and were reduced to hand wringing. Getting from the Copenhagen airport to Sweden without entering Denmark consumed my thinking for the remainder of the trip. Sending Major X back to England, and proceeding without him, wasn't really an acceptable alternative. It would leave the final assessment of the Hush House in the hands of only one man whose stance was uncertain.

I found an OAG (Official Airline Guide) on the airplane and began searching for alternatives. Four Hush House sites were selected for inspection. We could fly to Stockholm, reverse the direction of the trip once again and look at the more northern sites first. However, this would further upset the schedule the Swedes had rearranged, already delayed a day by Mr. Z's airplane problems. It would also leave Major X with no way to get back to the Copenhagen airport from southern Sweden, at the end of the trip.

More grinding through the OAG revealed a small, 'treetop' airline that ran a commuter flight from Copenhagen through Sweden, three days a week, with a stop in Malmo. However, the flights operated only Monday, Wednesday, and Friday, and this was Tuesday, courtesy of Mr. Z's delay. This was an off-day, but it gave me an idea.

Arriving in Malmo we met Agmen, whom I knew well. I explained the problem to him and asked him to keep Major X and Mr. Z busy. I left them in a mode of 'woe is me,' while I went to the counter of the small airline.

Again, I was in luck. Although it was an 'off-day for the commuter airline, and no counter personnel were present, I found an airline manager of some sort in a back room and explained my problem. After some negotiating I managed to cut an inexpensive deal for a 'charter trip' to Malmo early the next day, a flight of about 15 miles. My luck got even better; I found the manager was also a pilot and flew an occasional trip for the airline. After I explained our complications for the following day, he offered to immediately load us into an unused Twin Otter and transport us from our Copenhagen 'no-man's-land' to Sweden. I returned to our group, collected Agmen, Major X and Mr. Z, and we were off for Malmo, a flight of about five minutes across the Oresund, hardly leaving the Copenhagen Airport's traffic pattern.

On the ground in Sweden, we caught a cab to the ferry terminal, where Agmen had left his car, but then another problem reared its head: potential contractor gratuities.

Another Annoyance

During the cab trip, Mr. Z decided that if the word got back to his management that he accepted transportation from a potential contractor, it could be judged as a 'gratuity,' so the two Air Force people couldn't ride in Agmen's car. We solved this difficulty by finding a rental car for the military contingent. They rode separately, in a taxi, to the car rental agency, while Agmen and I followed in Agmen's car. Finally, we were off for a hotel in Helsingborg, with Agmen leading the way: four people in a two-car caravan but following all the military and legal jots and tittles. It had been a long day; fortunately, Helsingborg was only a short drive north from Malmo.

Sweden by Lamplight

Sweden in December, is not a very thrilling place. It's *dark*. Our caravan got an early start for Swedish Air Force Base at Angelholm, the location of the first Hush House facility, where we arrived before sunrise. In winter, dawn struggles at these latitudes, arriving sometime around 10:00 AM. Kipling's poem, "The Road To Mandalay," tells us:

"An' the dawn comes up like thunder outer China 'crost the Bay," but Sweden in December is not Mandalay. The sun works hard for its place in the day.

When we arrived at Angelholm, the Swedes put on a good show. The "Stars And Stripes" was flying over the base, along with the Swedish flag. Inside, the test facility was tastefully decorated with more American Flags. Even the hangar's door bell was programmed to play "The Star Spangled Banner."

We watched a test run of a Saab J-35 Draken and inspected the muffler tube as soon as it cooled. Then we were treated to a formal luncheon with the base commander. After some closing conversation with the technical staff the caravan departed, in the dark once again. The sun yields to night shortly after 2:00 PM in December.

It was nearly nine pm when we arrived in Vasteras, the site of the original Hush House. It was a drive of more than 300 miles, about six hours. Since this facility had been in use for almost 15 years, it was of particular interest to Mr. Z and Major X. Inspection of the muffler tube revealed only three or four small welds, to repair cracks, since the facility was inaugurated.

Swedish Viggen

We left Vasteras in early afternoon with a wee bit of daylight left, but covered the distance to Linkoping – pronounced 'Linchirping;' please don't ask about Swedish phonetics – mostly in the dark. It was another long drive, doubling back over much the trail covered the prior day, an inconvenience made necessary by the schedule changes. We visited the Hush House at Linkoping, in the dark of the following morning, watched the test of a Viggen and then on to another, at close-by Norkoping ('Norchirping') in the afternoon. We drove in the dark to Stockholm, for the night.

Agmen arranged interesting accommodations for the night: a cabin on a sailing vessel anchored in Stockholm Harbor. The boat was a real curiosity; U.S. tobacco heiress Doris Duke once owned it. It was a sizable boat with its own, compact, on-board restaurant and a fine menu.

The next day, a Saturday, was given over to an all day review of the Hush House inspection trip. Both Mr. Z and Major X were well pleased with the results of our whirlwind tour around Sweden, and they were convinced of the technical superiority and longevity of the Hush House concept. However, for much of the day, Mr. Z was on the Air Force grapevine and had discovered there had been a major reorganization that might impinge on our program.

Upheaval

General Bellis, a key to our program in U.S. Air Force Europe, had been replaced. Sgt. Graham got into some kind of trouble for speaking out too forcefully in a meeting and was relieved of his posting. Sgt. Nettles at TAC was replaced, circumstances unknown. An upcoming noise suppressor conference, at which the General, Nettles and Graham were to speak, was a shamble, and we would have to go about reconstructing much of the complex political apparatus we had put in place. Late in the day, Mr. Z departed Stockholm directly to the U.S., while Major X and I boarded a flight to London.

What had been a successful trip was darkened by this sudden cloud. Our carefully assembled machine was in need of repair, and with so little information, we didn't know where to start.

Another Strange Tack

Once we were airborne for London, I was looking forward to a nap, but Maj. X wanted to talk. We puzzled over the strange events discovered by Mr. Z. Without really knowing anything useful, it was a fitful, somewhat useless conversation.

Shifting the course of the conversation, Major X suddenly said,

"Why don't you come to London for the rest of the weekend? You could stay at my house. Tomorrow, my wife and I are taking our daughter into London to see the Christmas decorations; you could join us." I declined politely, deferring to the Christmas Season and my desire to get home. More inane conversation ensued for quite some time, when Major X let go another zinger.

"You really ought to see London at Christmas. The whole city is brightly decorated. You shouldn't miss it." Again, I declined, but the pressure continued. Fortunately, dinner was served, bringing the uncomfortable discussion to a temporary close.

On our final approach into London Heathrow, Major X made one more push that revealed his whole subterranean plan.

"Look," he said, "I don't want to write this d*** trip report. Won't you please spend a day or two at my house and write it for me?" Well now, that changed my thinking. Recalling the success I had had with Graham's report, I reluctantly accepted. We spent a few minutes together Saturday night drafting an outline, and I spent Sunday at Major X's kitchen table, grinding out the European Theater's final report on the Swedish trip, in longhand. Major X, his wife and daughter went into London to look at the Christmas decorations. By mining Major X's refrigerator, I made my own lunch, which I shared with Major X's dog.

On Monday, we went to Major X's office at RAF Mildenhall to get the report typed. After proof reading it, Major X dropped me off at London Heathrow, where I found my flight to be nine hours late. I managed to change my flight arrangements and grabbed an overnight flight to Washington, to talk to Maj. Capps and assess the damage to our fragile, political machine.

10

Shifting Gears

The technology issues were napping, at least for now. It was largely a political game from here.

*   *   *

Back in Washington, the situation didn't seem nearly as bad as conjured up by the terrors wrought of remoteness. Major Capps didn't assign disaster status to the problems resulting from staff changes in USAFE and TAC. He felt the Hush House program had built up a sufficient momentum of its own by then, so the shuffle of people wouldn't likely affect it much. And on Capitol Hill, Vento's assistant had managed to keep the program 'above the line' (see appendix: "Building the Budget") in both the House of Representatives and Senate budget bills. It appeared the 'new money' he was shepherding through the 1980 Budget, when added to the 'out year' money Capps had 'stolen' from the water-cooled suppressor program, would total about $40 million.

With things going so well in Washington, I caught an afternoon flight for San Antonio to attend to some loose ends, which had unraveled while I was gone. At the time, I wasn't aware I was facing a variety of conflicting events and interests that would consume almost a year of weekly shuttling between home, Washington, Dayton and San Antonio, with an occasional run to Europe. ASE was in the 'cat-bird seat.' It was now holding a Federal Stock Number for the Hush House, which we had negotiated prior to the Coningsby tests. There were, however, a variety of competing and sometimes conflicting interests and cross-currents to be satisfied, before a contract could be signed. To review:

- A sole-source contract is anathema to government agencies. Competition is the watchword, and ASE's Federal Stock Number assured it would be the only source of air-cooled test facilities for several years.

- ASE wanted a large enough contract to justify setting up a manufacturing facility, which implied a contract large enough to attract the attention of the industry press, with all the complications a bright light might bring.

- U.S. Air Force Europe (USAFE) wanted six air-cooled units NOW, but six units would not justify the establishment of a new manufacturing facility. USAFE's needs would have to be satisfied as part of a larger whole – another selling job.

- There was no hope of slipping something through 'under the radar' because the projected $40 million contract would be, at the time, the largest Air Force contract ever awarded for ground support equipment. But I wasn't aware of that.

- The Air Force's Research and Development group at Wright-Patterson would be drastically reduced or eliminated by the adoption of the Hush House. There would no longer be a need for the design, development and moving of airplane-specific noise suppressors.

- In desperation, competitors submitted a last-minute, unsolicited proposals for their own air-cooled test facilities.

- The 'equipment' vs. 'facilities' dilemma: Mixing money of differing 'colors' was unusual and attracted attention.

- The Sole Source Dilemma: An unforeseen problem resulting from the agreement to assign a Federal Stock Number to the Hush House after the Coningsby tests.

A Game Of Cat & Mouse

The demise of the alleged 'competitive' status, enjoyed by the two producers of water cooled noise suppressors, eliminated a decades-old comfortable operating structure. There was no Hush House competitor, and there wasn't any other potential supplier with a Federal Stock Number. This resulted in great consternation inside the San Antonio Air Logistics Center's (SAALC) procurement function. The problem was assigned to a 'Buyer' functionary at SAALC, in whose office I found myself for discussion of the foregoing issues.

The 'sole-source' status of ASE regarding the procurement, had obviously been rattling around the procurement office for some time. Legal authorities decided that the only way to alleviate the stigma associated with a sole-source procurement, would be for the Air Force to acquire the manufacturing rights to the Swedish Hush House design, which could facilitate an open procurement.

At this point, I was supposed to be blind to everything going on in the background. The Buyer was too far removed from back room, day-to-day activities to know I had been driving the entire program from San Antonio to Washington, Germany and England. Not only was I familiar with most of the nasty internal Air Force cross-currents, but I also knew how much money the Buyer was playing with because I had assembled his budget.

The Buyer began without preliminaries; he didn't even open his voluminous file folder.

"What would it cost to buy the technical rights to the design and manufacturing data for the Hush House?" I wasn't prepared for that question, just then. I didn't know whether the Swedes would want to sell the design, but it flashed through my mind that anything is for sale if the price is right. I knew Olof thought if we were awarded a program for $5 million, he would think he had landed on the moon. With the knowledge that between Maj. Capps' out-year money and what I was working on in the Congress, we would have about $40 million in the in the bank, and probably a bit more to potentially build 25 facilities, I decided to take the problem head-on.

Allowing for Olof's clear $5 million, plus a little negotiating room, I picked a number out of the air. After a studied hesitation, I replied,

"Oh, I suppose the Swedes would want somewhere in the neighborhood of $50 million. There's the loss of profits stemming from proprietary advantage in future business worldwide, and of course, the sunk cost of all the initial design and testing must be considered." The Buyer seemed a bit taken aback, but he knew the number I had given him wasn't ridiculously out of the budget range. He was obviously aware of some events transpiring in Washington.

*   *   *

The normal way of buying a system such as the Hush House would be for the Air Force to write a 'Requirement' specification, solicit design ideas from a number of vendors, and award a competitive development contract to one winning competitor. The winner would build a *'first article'* for test and evaluation, which, if successful, would result in the assigning of a Federal Stock Number to the approved design. The Air Force would then own the design, having paid the initial winner for its design and construction of the 'first article.' Succeeding systems would be purchased by putting the detailed drawings and specifications 'on the street' for anyone to bid on competitively. We upset this process by pre-negotiating for a Federal Stock Number, to be awarded as result of the successful Coningsby tests. ASE owned the FSN and the whole game, at this point. The Buyer was attempting to gain ownership of the design and data, so that the Hush House would thereafter fit into the procurement system.

*   *   *

The Buyer countered,

"Suppose the Air Force were to buy one Hush House and erect it here in San Antonio. What would the design data cost when combined with the hardware?"

"Oh, I suppose $45 million," I replied."

"Well, suppose we bought five systems. Then what would the data cost?"

"Maybe ... about $35 million," I replied, "but we would have to take a closer look at the construction cost of the five systems," I answered, working the mental arithmetic to preserve Olof and ASE a clean, $5 million windfall, instead of a total sale of $5 million, which I knew was Olof's pipe dream, but this free-wheeling cat & mouse game had the numbers floating all over the playground. To give downstream negotiating room, I tossed in:

"Of course, this is all subject to approval of ASE management and the Swedes, who know nothing about this conversation. I'm not authorized to speak for the company, officially."

We played this game through several iterations, and the buyer seemed dismayed that whatever he proposed, the total number always came out to about $50 million; there would be time to yield toward $40 million later. The really hard, definitive negotiation came months later, but as this conversation ended I knew that with some care and feeding and a little luck, I was on the way to a $40 million contract. I had no concept of how long it would take. This was another fresh, new map with no lines on it.

ASE's Long-Term Objectives

ASE's position as a sole-source contractor, with its unique Federal Stock Number, quickly became entangled with the Air Force's urgent need to replace the existing test facilities and to also satisfy government policy regarding competitive procurement considerations. With the wide interest being exhibited by Air Force Operations across the Western Hemisphere, ASE's ambitions had expanded from a few units built by sub-contractors, as their earlier engine-only test cells were built. The company was now looking toward to setting up a company-owned manufacturing operation to support the contract. We determined this would require a quantity order for about 25 or more Hush Houses. The work by Major Capps, and the funding we were assembling in Congress, made that a vivid 'carrot' and a real possibility.

Internal Air Force procurement concerns were creating problems with a contract of this size. Air Force buyers were fearful of attracting explorations by outside publicity agents – such as the television show "Sixty Minutes". The extreme pressures being exerted by U.S. Air Forces Europe, for immediate delivery of six units, were in conflict with ASE's need for more systems to justify a new manufacturing facility. Thus, the requirement for purchase of the 'rights and data' was not palatable to ASE with only a six-unit purchase.

Wright Patterson Research & Development Command

Lurking in the background was the Wright-Patterson R&D function, interested in preserving proprietary 'ownership' over this next generation test facility. It threatened to severely truncate their engineering activity, dedicated to designing and moving custom-fitted airplane test cells around the world. While the R&D group's interests had been effectively 'overcome by events,' as the British would say, they never missed an opportunity to push for a prolonged development program, under their own auspices. They got their best shot at involvement, when both manufacturers of water-cooled mufflers submitted unsolicited proposals seeking to develop their own 'Hush Houses,' under a program to be funded by the Air Force.

Chaos broke out! The USAF European Commanding General went ballistic: He wanted his six Hush Houses IMMEDIATELY! The R&D Command's response was, in effect,

"You can't proceed with this sole-source procurement because there are now potential competitors." San Antonio Logistics Command's response, was to intensify the contract negotiations and to attempt to award a contract to ASE as soon as possible. It was a wild ride.

A 'Letter' Contract

San Antonio ALC's response to the unsolicited proposals, was to quickly offer ASE a 'letter contract' for 25 systems. While this had the sound of music, it could lead to a fatal trap. A letter contract carries no final price – perhaps only 'price 'targets,' if any – and commits the contractor to deliver the product to a tight specification, with a fixed schedule and the final price negotiated only after the product has been delivered. Further, the government determines, after the fact, precisely what costs of doing business the contractor will be allowed to include in the pricing of his product. Any profit the contractor might be allowed is also determined after the government has received the product. Depending on the people and relationships involved, the letter contract can be a ticket to corporate bankruptcy, or commitment to a mental institution for the operative contractor personnel. However, it was a tempting carrot, particularly for a small company anticipating a major government opportunity. In the end, we refused the letter contract and created an uproar in SAALC. They were counting on an eager little company 'taking the bait.'

The Buyer threatened to 'kill the whole thing.' That prompted a response out of Europe, threatening some unspecified internal Air Force mayhem. I was in over my head, and ASE sought the advice of an attorney specializing in government contracts, Dale Nathan. Dale was short of stature – a bit over four feet tall – but long on experience with government contracting. We often referred to him as our 'micro attorney.' Dale's watch words were,

"We're gonna zap 'em" and on several occasions, he did.

Dale reviewed our situation and came up with a potential solution. The worst terrors of a letter contract could be mitigated. By pre-negotiating the cost items the Air Force would allow in the final version of the contract, the risk could be reduced to an acceptable level but didn't eliminate it completely. He set out the areas of government procurement regulations where I could find the rules related to 'items of allowable cost' in a letter contract. No trivial task, this.

The Department of Defense purchasing regulations, originally inscribed on a few typewritten sheets, have expanded over the years to several hundred thousand pages, now printed on tissue-thin paper similar to the old family bible and bound in many volumes. With Dale's guidance, it took me several weeks to prepare a list of items we considered essential before we could consider a letter contract.

The Negotiation

Ultimately, I prepared a list of over 30 items of cost to be pre-negotiated for inclusion in a letter contract. About 20 of these were absolute 'deal breakers,' essential to any contract, another five were fairly important, and the remainder were expendable currency to accommodate the cooperative, give-and-take that must occur in any negotiation – throwaways, so to speak. These allow your opponent to 'win a few,' as a face-saving gesture. I sent the list to the Buyer in San Antonio, to serve as the basis for final negotiations leading to *the* contract. A date was set, and I headed off to San Antonio for what I expected would be a controversial meeting. I wasn't disappointed.

As a negotiating tactic I deliberately set the time of the meeting for a Friday afternoon at 3:00 PM, knowing San Antonio ALC would pretty well be wound-down for the weekend by late afternoon. The timing would inject an artificial urgency into the meeting. I met the Buyer in his office, assuming this would be the location for the meeting. By then, he had been involved with the program's details for nearly a year and was a well understood quantity. I was unconcerned about dealing with him.

Upon my arrival, he presented an unusually cordial mood, proba- bly anticipating his weekend activities, I concluded. Actually, he was likely contemplating his good fortune by escaping from this torturing problem. After a few pleasantries, he announced we would be meeting elsewhere, and we set off, walking nearly the full length of a building that approached a quarter mile in length. I noted to myself that consuming time at this point, was in my favor. Finally, we reached the area of the executive offices and entered a door marked 'Deputy Chief of Procurement.' Uh-oh, a ringer I hadn't counted on. A new face, no prior knowledge of a year's twists and turns and an unfamiliar psychological quantity. It boded ill.

*   *   *

In military organizations, 'Deputy' anyone, is usually a civilian with a theoretical boss, the 'Chief,' who is often a formal member of the military. The military occupant of the post usually rotates on a cycle of three or four years. The Deputy is the operative chief, with longer tenure in the office and is the possessor of the 'corporate memory' of the unit.

*   *   *

The Buyer introduced me to the Deputy Chief of Procurement, who responded with a frosty handshake, and the Buyer departed. The Deputy sat, motioned me to a chair opposite his desk and fired his first salvo.

"Look," he snarled, "I've looked at your stuff," motioning to my

list of 'allowable costs' on his desk, "You might as well take this sh**
and go back to Minneapolis. A \$40 million contract to a \$5 million
company has never happened before, and it ain't gonna happen now.
We can't agree to these cost items."

Nice opening, I thought. Not a good beginning, but I had seen
bluffers before, and I knew the real heat was on him, not me.

"So which items can't you allow?" I asked.

"None of 'em," he replied, gruffly, maintaining the bluff. I ignored
his shot and began with the obvious.

"Well, some of them are essential to conducting any business; let's
look at number one. Surely, you would allow the payment of sala-
ries?"

"Well, I suppose so, but this is a futile exercise," he responded.
Ignoring his comment, I checked off item number one, with a bit of
a flourish and continued.

"If you want these facilities built, you have to allow us to purchase
materials."

"Yeah, I suppose," he replied. I soldiered on through about a half
dozen items, without encountering a single snag, and then we hit a
problem, whose details I have long forgotten.

"Absolutely not," he said, banging his fist on his desk for emphasis. I shot back,

"If you open those books behind you, you will find this item is
specifically allowed: Volume 7, page 543, paragraph 4, sub-paragraph
c"(cited from memory, not an accurate reference). With a sigh and
grimaced disgust, he turned to the bookcase, housing the thousands
of pages of procurement regulations, which is standard-issue for his
sort. He selected a volume and leafed through the tissue pages with a
flourish, initially. He then settled in to really read the tiny print. After
perhaps 10 minutes, he turned around, shrugged and said,

"I suppose you can find most any damn thing in these things, if
you look long enough." I checked off item 7 on my list, knowing I
had won. It was approaching 4:30, and the weekend was looming.

The rest was easy. We ticked off the remaining items in my list, almost perfunctorily, with an occasional, despondent objection.

"Why don't you check your books again, Here's the reference paragraph number," I'd suggest.

"Nah, I'll give you that one," he'd reply; 5:00 p.m. was coming fast.

In the end, despite all the tension and trepidation, the big negotiation was a pushover. He approved all the items I needed for a contract and then some: 29 of the original 33. I lost only four of the throwaways. It was as though the Deputy Chief had just completed a tutorial class in negotiation and forgotten all the essentials. We walked out at 5:05, the best of friends. It was the weekend, after all.

However, he wasn't through with me yet; the worst trials were reserved for future months and did not shadow our genial parting that Friday afternoon. Perhaps, in my concealed elation, I didn't sense the foreboding in his parting words. As we shook hands he warned,

"Look," he said, "you 'gotta' change the name of this thing. Hush House sounds like the name of a 'no-tell' motel in the wrong part of town."

11

The Shoot-Out At GAO

Once again, it's never over until it's over.

* * *

A s we sat back, satisfied the job was done, and we only had to wait for contract papers to be presented for signatures, termites began to appear in our foundation. The old water-cooled test cell companies, plus another previously unknown player, submitted protests to the General Accounting Office, challenging the potential award of a sole-source contract to ASE. This elevated all the wrangling to whole new level of government.

The GAO is the final authority in contractual disputes such as

these. I immediately went from a position, where I knew all the players and had a modicum of control of the situation, to a new game
that was almost legally impenetrable. The GAO usually operated behind closed doors, deliberating in private and rendering a decision on
its own time schedule, somewhat akin to the Supreme Court. Gloom
descended on the Air Force and in turn, on ASE. However, Olof,
with victory within his grasp, was not to be denied. He suggested I
schedule a meeting with our micro attorney and flew in from Philadelphia to attend.

Dale Nathan was pretty depressed over this turn of events. He
suggested we contact a Washington legal firm, Schnader, Harrison,
Segal & Lewis, which specialized in government contracting issues. It
was one of the firms featured in a popular business book of the time,
"The Super Lawyers." By a lucky draw, my first call to the firm drew
a response from Paul Dembling, whose long record of working with
government agencies showed him to be ideally suited for our current
problem. There was no searching around. Paul was 'it' from the first
call.

These days, with Google's capability, a search on Paul G. Dembling produces more than 3000 citations. The following introduction,
from a NASA publication, gives a small bit of Paul's background. He
emerged to be one of those providential intersections with my life's
trajectory.

> *Present at the Creation: Paul G. Dembling, Author of NASA's
> Founding Legislation*
> *By Edward S. Goldstein, Gregory C. La Rosa and David S.
> Schuman*
> *NASA's founding can be credited to a number of figures, some famous
> like President Dwight D. Eisenhower, who determined that a civilian agency
> should lead America's space exploration efforts, then-Senate majority leader
> Lyndon B. Johnson, who pushed for a strong American effort in space.
> Behind the scenes, people like Paul G. Dembling, general counsel to the
> National Advisory Committee for Aeronautics (NACA) and later
> NASA, and Johnson's legislative aides Eilene Galloway and Glenn
> Wilson, helped to shape NASA's legislative charter, the National*

Aeronautics and Space Act of 1958. In this compilation of two interviews, Dembling, who also ran NASA's Legislative Affairs Office under Administrator James Webb, discussed his role in drafting the Space Act and other major events he witnessed. Dembling is now retired and living in Florida.

Even more to the point, after his service with NASA, Paul was Chief Counsel for the General Accounting Office and a mentor for its then-current Chief Counsel. While Paul was too ethical to use his role to apply overt pressure, he could insert added background and detail directly to the Chief Counsel, his successor, and ascertain how the winds were blowing on the Hush House protest. He simply had reasons to be around the GAO from time to time without an invitation, so the right contacts could 'just happen.'

The GAO opened its review of the Hush House case by requesting a written brief, stating our position, within 30 days. Dembling had been through many protests, such as I the one was facing, from the other side of the desk and knew exactly what was expected in the required paper submissions. He coached me through the preparation of a legal brief he would use as the basis for a final document. As with all such tasks, after the first draft is completed everyone involved has a variation on the original theme, and the task tends to fill the entire time allowed against a hard deadline. A couple of days before the deadline, I was off for Washington to deliver the document to Dembling, for polishing and addition of the proper legal syntax. Despite a lot of Air Force pressure on the GAO, this was not going to be a quick process. The lines went dead for almost 10 months.

And In the Background

Back in San Antonio ALC, there was somewhat feverish activity. U.S. Air Force Europe applied pressure on the procurement people to proceed to a contract without waiting for the GAO decision. While the procurement function resisted this pressure and ultimately attempted to scuttle the whole program, I continued my efforts to get the required funding into the Congressional Budget for fiscal year

1980. Several crucial factors began to take shape just before government's fiscal year ended on September 30, 1979. The Buyer for the procurement began to cave under the internal pressure and called a major meeting, involving most of the interested parties, and it was back to San Antonio once again. Although the meeting was widely attended by various interests from Washington, Dayton and Germany, the Buyer opened the meeting with a 17-word admonition:

"This meeting would not be occurring without forces originating outside this office. The meeting is now adjourned." As with many forced actions, the 30-second meeting satisfied only the order that the meeting be held but was a waste of time and travel money.

I never comprehended what drove the animosity of the procurement function, except that the Hush House program was undoubtedly an anomaly, which didn't fit the system. First of all, the fact that it was a sole-source procurement was an immediate red flag. There was no other competitor with an equivalent product, and Air Force Operations wanted it, but that really didn't help. The contract's size was also a problem, and San Antonio ALC was laboring under an imaginary cloud, fearful that a team of media investigative reporters would turn up in their offices, momentarily.

So we waited helplessly for the GAO to complete its review and render a decision. Several weeks after my show-down negotiation with the Deputy Chief of Procurement, I received a call from the Buyer, who took new tack. He began with:

"The DCAS (Defense Contract Administration Service)Team has recommended 'no contract' in your case because of the financial inadequacy of ASE and its lack of a computerized accounting system. I can give you three months to comply with the accounting system, even after contract award, but there is no way the financial capability of ASE will ever justify the award of a contract of this size." He seemed somewhat pleased with his announcement. I didn't realize, at this point, that if it were awarded, the Hush House contract would be the largest 'Ground Support Equipment' contract ever awarded by the Air Force up to that time, a real anomaly. I replied,

"We have already addressed that problem and arranged a $3 million line of credit with a Philadelphia bank" – Olof secured the line of credit through his past relationship with the bank and the backing of Granges-Nyby in Sweden. The Buyer seemed disappointed at the news. After some discussion, he said, in effect,

'*We never thought you could do that.*'

The phone line with San Antonio was quiet for a week or two; then the Buyer called again.

"When you did your analysis of the cash required to get a manufacturing facility up and running, I'll bet you did your analysis as a Small Business."

"Well, of course," I replied, "ASE meets all the Small Business requirements: sales volume, number of employees, etc." The Buyer countered,

"Why don't you rework your cash requirements analysis as Large Business, and get back to me? Maybe you can be classified as a Large Business because you are a subsidiary of a large Swedish Company." Despite my objections, he terminated the conversation abruptly.

"Do your analysis as a Large Business, and get back to me."

The difference between a Small and a Large Business may seem trivial, but in reality it could result in a financial disaster. Unfortunately, it was one consideration I hadn't included in developing the list of allowable costs we negotiated earlier.

As a Small Business, a contractor can bill the government for *committed* purchases, i.e. purchased material or equipment to be used in fulfilling a contract but not yet delivered to the government. As a Large Business, the contractor can bill the government only for items and material *actually delivered to the government.*

With the Hush Houses this was significant because of all the steel that went into the structure. The material might take six months, or even a year, to go through the process of procurement, fabrication, delivery to Europe and final erection of the facility. ASE would have to shoulder the cost burden over the entire period, if it were adjudged to be a Large Business. As a Small Business, ASE could bill the government for material immediately upon ordering from the steel mill, and it might be many months or more from ordering to delivery to ASE. During that time, if the government paid the bill expeditiously, ASE could retain the money, with interest, while the steel order was running through the mill and fabrication by ASE. The difference between Small and Large Business rules, nearly doubled the required capital.

Upon completing our analysis, I called the Buyer and relayed the results.

"That's about what we thought," he replied, "And further, we have a judgment from the JAG Office (Judge Adjutant General) says you are a Large Business for purposes of this contract. Are you going to be able to raise that kind of money?"

"I'll have to look at our options and get back to you," I said. Then he dropped the load of bricks on my head.

"I'll give you a week to get your funding in order," and hung up.

I wondered at the precipitous deadline, thinking it might be punitive but then realized he was likely dealing with some internal deadline related to the imminent end of the government's fiscal year.

I immediately called Olof in Pennsylvania and discussed this inconvenient development. It was a Thursday afternoon, and it was time for Olof to do 'his thing.' Olof dropped everything else on his agenda and said,

"I'll go to Sweden tonight and talk to Ole Lund (the Managing Director of Granges-Nyby) tomorrow."

Olof was not going to be denied at this point and was going all-out for the Air Force contract. We had several telephone conversations over the weekend regarding the art of the possible. Lund called a weekend emergency meeting of Granges' Board of Directors, and Olof returned to the U.S. early Monday morning with a guarantee for $6 million. I called the Buyer in San Antonio with the news. My elation may not have been well hidden, but his response didn't reflect jubilation at our good fortune; a short conversation ensued, the essence of which was,

'*We never thought you could do that.*'

Just before lunch the Buyer called back; he was going to take one last shot at us.

"The $6 million, how can the government be assured ASE will use that money only for the Hush House program and not to shore up ASE's own finances or to retire current liabilities?" It was a valid question. It was obvious there were a lot of conversations going on in San Antonio between phone calls. More than one head was working on 'their problem.' I responded by suggesting we would set up a separate corporation whose sole function would be to hold the $6 million and execute the Hush House contract. I had no time to discuss this with anyone, and it was just a half-baked idea, suggested in desperation.

"I think that would work, but I'll give you until the close of business Friday to get that done," came the reply. There was a certain tone of glee in his acquiescence; it was obvious he thought he had killed the program. He thought it would be impossible to set up a corporation in less than a week. However, there was a certain logic in his deadline: Friday was the 28th of September, the last working day of fiscal year 1979.

I relayed the latest development to Olof, with a suggestion: I had incorporated my consulting practice in Texas a few months before and had an established relationship with an agent who might be able to expeditiously create a Texas corporation. Texas was a favorable tax state, and with San Antonio being the center of contractual action it made sense to have a Texas-based subsidiary. Further, after months of study, we had isolated Texas and Georgia as suitable sites for a fabrication company. It made no sense to heat the expansive spaces required to fabricate the large acoustic sub-structures in Minnesota. Olof approved the idea of a Texas corporation.

I called the agent I had used to incorporate some months earlier and set out my problem to him, emphasizing the urgent schedule we were being forced to meet. This was before the days of FedEx and email, so moving signatures and money around, by first-class mail, was going to be a problem, with only four days to meet the deadline. I could act as a personal courier, if necessary; after all we had been through, what was one more trip?

The minimum capitalization for a Texas corporation was $1000, and the filing fee was $100 so it wasn't a matter of money but of time.

"I think we can do it," the agent said, "for an extra fee, I can expedite the paper work by walking it through the State House and complete the incorporation steps in a couple of hours."

"How much is the expediting fee," I asked?

"Well, I haven't done a walk-through for a while, but it was $10 the last I remember. I'll fax you the forms right now; you can sign them and fax them back, so I can start the process this afternoon," the agent suggested. Because of my former relationship with him, he volunteered to put up the $1110 himself, if we'd wire the money to him the following day. Done.

All went well, without the usual snags, which often occur when the chips are down, and by noon Tuesday "ASE Texas Incorporated" was a reality. The agent put the executed papers in a counter-to-counter service airlines provided before the days of UPS, and we had the required documentation by late afternoon on Tuesday.

On Wednesday morning, I faxed a copy of the certificate of incorporation to the Buyer. Upon receipt, he called immediately and said,

"Damn! We never thought you could do that." He capitulated, and we were back on the path to a contract.

Having been completely entangled in the minute by minute details of getting the job done, I hadn't reflected on the irony of what was happening. The Air Force procurement people, obsessively concerned with ASE's small size, and how it might default on the impending contract, went to extremes in trying to avoid consummating the contract with such a small company. Now, with a bit of time to ponder what had transpired in the past few days, I realized the Air Force was proceeding to a $39 million contract with 'ASE Texas Incorporated,' a company that had:

No building
No manufacturing capability
No machinery
No material inventory
$1000 capitalization
And only one employee: me

The last item was corrected in a few days when ASE hired John Copeland who was then the Vice President of Field Operations for my old client, Brown Minneapolis Tank. John was a Texan and eager to return to home ground.

A Hearing at General Accounting Office Headquarters

We were now back in the waiting game; it appeared all hurdles had been overcome, but the shadow of the GAO investigation remained. However, the distant drums seemed to carry the message of a favorable outcome.

With the location of ASE Texas generally determined, John Copeland embarked on the task of weighing the most suitable and generous solicitations from small Texas towns to entice the company to locate in their community. After evaluating several offers, John chose the town of Crockett, named after Texas folk hero Davy Crockett, as the location for ASE Texas. He put down a small holding fee and signed an option giving us a few months to wait out the GAO decision. The site had a rudimentary building and sufficient acreage to allow for the storage of materials and work in process.

The Shoot-Out At GAO

In what was apparently an unusual development, the GAO called for a formal hearing on the protests they had received. This was all new ground for me, and even Paul Dembling admitted preparation was difficult. The twists and turns, which we might encounter in such a free-wheeling shoot-out among antagonists, were unpredictable. I put together as much material as I could conveniently carry and set out for Washington.

The hearing was held at GAO Headquarters, in a very small, poorly ventilated room, with barely enough space to allow chairs to be placed around a small table. There were about a dozen people in the room: two from GAO, the three protesters, each with two lawyers, a gentleman we will call Mr. Y, Paul Dembling and me.

After introductions all around, complete with an occasional snide remark about the size and capability of ASE, it was evident this wasn't likely to be a pleasant exercise. They might as well have passed around a tray with brass knuckles and said, 'Go to it!' It was, perhaps, the most high-pressure situation I had ever been in. I was glad to have Paul Dembling with me because it appeared we were off on a legal path, given all the lawyers present.

Mr Y's presence in this group was strange and unexpected. I had met him once before, in a Navy meeting on engine testing. He displayed an unlikeable personality and had dominated the meeting with an arrogant assertion of his views, supported with little technical substance. As best I could tell, he was an architect of sorts and had designed an enclosed, acoustical hangar for the Navy at Miramar Naval Air Station, near San Diego. How he got invited to this meeting was never explained. Perhaps the third protester retained him as a 'technical expert.'

The investigator from GAO set the stage by summarizing the reasons for meeting and called on the protesting firms, in alphabetical order, to state their objections. Given the plethora of legal considerations involved and professional makeup of the individual teams, I expected to be engaged in a legally based debate, for which I was ill prepared. To my astonishment, the first company's lawyer took aim with an argument based on physics and engineering principles, for which *he* was ill prepared. I took notes and kept silent, waiting for the proper opportunity to strike.

The GAO investigator, inadvertently helped our position in responding to the lawyer. He pointed out that the high operating temperatures, combined with water and sulfur in the fuel, caused such severe corrosion problems that the water-cooled suppressors required overhaul after only two to three years of service, instead of their 'guaranteed' six-year life. The countering argument presented was that the Air Force specification required the use of 'mild steel' construction, and if the specifications were changed to allow stainless steel they would be able to meet the six-year life requirement, at an added cost, of course.

The second protester took up where the first left off, presenting a muddled argument on the merits of water vs. air-cooling. Reduced to its elements, he argued the specification should never be changed to allow air cooling because air is physically incapable of matching water as a coolant. Paul Dembling, who said nothing up to this point, jumped into the fray, pointing out that one of these firms wants the specification changed while the other does not.

"Look, gentlemen," he said, "you can't have it both ways. Either you want the specification changed or you don't. You'll have to get together, and make up your minds." It was a brilliant point I had missed, while consumed with the technical jousting. Our position began to look somewhat easier than it appeared at the outset.

The third firm was then called to state its case. Their lawyer immediately deferred to Mr. Y who chose to focus his attack not on fundamental physics but on the ASE proposed facility itself:

"The airplanes in use in Europe are second rate," he began. "They're mostly obsolete and with small engines, but the U.S. Air Force flies airplanes whose engines run hotter and produce more thrust." He cited the F-15, with its Pratt & Whitney F-100 engine, as one whose exhaust efflux was beyond air-cooling, as proposed for eSE's Hush House. Continuing, he went on to allege that the Pratt & Whitney TF-30 engine, in the F-111 fighter bomber, was the nastiest engine in existence, stating unequivocally, it would burn down the ASE facility in less than a minute. He presented neither analytical evidence nor test data. Now it was my turn.

"My presentation will be short," I began. "It is based on tests conducted in an air-cooled Hush House, at Royal Air Force Base Coningsby, in England. First, the F-100 engine; as you will note from this chart, is similar in thrust and fuel flow, to the Swedish RM-8 engine in the Saab Viggen, flown by the Swedish Air Force. It has been calibrated and tested for over 10 years, in the Hush House at Linkoping, Sweden. Last December, U.S. Air Force representatives inspected this facility and several similar facilities, for evidence of damage or repair, and they found them all in satisfactory condition. Further, testing of the F-100, both on a test stand and in the F-15 fighter aircraft, was conducted in a Hush House at RAF Coningsby in September 1978, along with a McDonnell-Douglas RF-4 and a General Dynamics F-111." I then displayed an 8 x 10 photograph of the F-100 running in the Coningsby Hush House, with a glowing afterburner flame extending down the muffler tube.

"This is the U.S. Air Force's most advanced engine running on a test stand at RAF Coningsby. The test data were acquired over a half-day's running without evidence of damage. Then, holding a picture of the F-111 running at Coningsby, I continued.

"Not only did the facility survive, but following the thrust stand tests of the F-100 and the TF-30, thermal data were measured in the muffler tube with the F-111 aircraft. Some tests were done with both TF-30 engines running, one of them in afterburner mode. This is the engine Mr. Y warns will 'burn down' the ASE proposed facility in less than a minute. Are there any questions?" There were none; the room went completely silent. The GAO inspector adjourned the meeting; we all shook hands and departed. Mr. Y refused to shake my hand and sullenly walked out of the room alone.

So, it was over. I felt we had made our point; there was nothing more we could do but await the final decision.

The Demise of Olof Muten

Shortly after the GAO shoot-out, news came that Olof, pursuing one of his two leisure pastimes, had an accident near his farm in Eastern Pennsylvania. While Olof was riding to hounds on a fox-hunt, his horse stopped suddenly at a jump but Olof didn't. Vaulting over the neck of the horse, he landed on his head and suffered what turned out to be irreparable brain damage. The watch was now on for two critical issues: the GAO decision and the recovery of Olof. We made-out better with the GAO than with Olof.

Ten days after Olof's accident, we received a call from Paul Dembling, saying the GAO decision upheld the Air Force's position; a sole-source contract with ASE was justified, under the circumstances and given the information provided to them. Olof, on the other hand, never really recovered from his brain injury, but there was a small bit of levity associated with his regaining a low level of consciousness.

Olof was always on the phone – he would have loved cell phones – and after he had been comatose for weeks, someone beside his hospital bed joked grimly that this was the longest he had ever gone without making a phone call. Another person impulsively picked up the telephone from the bedside table and placed it on Olof's stomach. To everyone's astonishment, Olof sat up immediately and started dialing the phone. Subsequently, he became semi-lucid and ate without a feeding tube, but I'm not sure he ever fully grasped that we had won the contract he was so dedicated to winning.

I got one laboriously handwritten letter from him, some months after his 'awakening,' but it was not totally coherent. It was a sad ending to a wonderful business relationship. After our stormy beginning, he had thoughtfully considered my view of our problems and backed every decision and action I took in his absence. I couldn't have asked for more.

Finally, A Contract

It was a close call, as were many things associated with the Hush House. After 39 months of intricate maneuvering, we were in yet another deadline-watch over which we had no control. The GAO decision occurred on February 21 of 1980, and the option on the manufacturing facility expired on the last day of February. There was a bit of scurrying about with paperwork in San Antonio, but finally the contract was ready. John Copeland and I flew to San Antonio on February 27 and John signed the $39 million contract at noon. We immediately went to the San Antonio Airport, where I rented a Cessna 172, and we flew to Crockett. John exercised the option on the manufacturing site, two days early – the leap year gave us a small, added cushion. Now all we had to do was gather machinery optioned with dealers around the country, build a functioning company and begin manufacturing Hush Houses.

Cleanup

There were a few odd and ends for me to finish before I could move on to other things. There were a couple of trips to England, to help choose locations for facilities at RAF bases near Mildenhall and Lakenheath. Mildenhall was a special problem; we had to choose a location and orientation that would minimize the noise propagation in the direction of Lord Someone-or-other's farm. As a Member of Parliament he had real political clout, and it was essential that the aircraft noise not disturb his prize-winning rabbits. It made no difference what the acoustic data would show; this was to be another version of the 'rabbit test.'

Later, I visited USAFE Headquarters at Ramstein to assure the USAFE Commanding General that we would do our best to deliver his Hush Houses immediately after the completion of the 'first item' tests at San Antonio. Back in San Antonio, there remained several months of coordination on small details, the fire suppression system, instrumentation and tie-down arrangements for various aircraft and for the M-37 test stand, used to test engines not installed in airframes.

I made one last trip to Washington to thank Major Capps and a few other people, for all the assistance afforded me over more than three years. I stopped for a moment to peer into General Bond's old office and gave silent tribute to the man who initially pulled the levers that made our success possible. Fittingly, it was empty. His successor was 'on travel.'

I told Major Capps that I was going to miss his can-do spirit and his 'never say die' attitude in those many times when it appeared as though we were finished. Capps replied that it had been an interesting ride, and he was glad that we finally prevailed.

He then mused that we needn't say goodbye quite yet. He was working with a company in Canada that needed the sort of help I could provide. They were encountering problems similar to those endured by ASE while working within the U.S. Department of Defense procurement system. He gave me a contact number that I called. That call resulted in job lasted nine years. It made the Hush House program look easy.

12

Building And Documentation

Sooner or later you might build something.

*   *   *

After signing the contract, John Copeland moved to Crockett, Texas and expeditiously gave life to ASE Texas. Meanwhile, my job being done, I took Major Capps' suggestion and called the 'little company in Canada' that needed my help. On first contact, I learned their problem with the U.S. Defense Establishment was also rooted in the San Antonio Air Logistics Center. Then the Air Force announced that the first Hush House would be built at Kelly Air Force Base in San Antonio, where it would be under the watchful eyes of the Air Logistics Center (SAALC), located at the base. ASE had selected Crockett, Texas to be near (SAALC), and the selection was even more fortuitous for me, given the site chosen for the first facility. Life was turning into a Texas world.

The building ASE leased from the city of Crockett was in a state of some disrepair, but John was able to quickly hire help and refurbish the site. He also acquired the used metal working machines that we had previously located, negotiated their purchase and moved them to Crockett. This he accomplished in a very short time. He was able to set up the Crockett operation, hire staff and produce the components for the first complete Hush House in about seven months.

Yet Another Wrinkle

Once the contract papers were signed, I did not expect to be involved with the execution of the contract, but the Air Force changed the plan for reasons rooted in money, as usual.

Government money has many colors, not all of them shades of green. In our case, the money inserted into the 1980 Department of Defense Budget was allocated to accounts dedicated to permanent structures, commonly called MCP money (Military Construction Program). On the other hand, the money Major Capps had reprogrammed from the out-year, water-cooled noise suppressors, was designated 'Equipment' funding.

The basic difference between 'Construction' and 'Equipment' is that 'Construction' (MCP) implies a permanent building, while 'Equipment' is capable of being dismantled and moved. So, ignoring the fact Hush Houses were unlikely to be moved within the lifespan of a steel building, it was decreed that the U.S. Air Force Hush Houses must be Equipment, i.e. movable. This required the basic Swedish design be altered, to allow the originally welded structure to be bolted together for easy disassembly. The large acoustical panels were subdivided to fit into shipping containers for ocean travel and trucking over standard roads and under bridges. These and other last-minute changes, plus the cost of the manufacturing license, turned a $39 million contract into a $49 million contract, a significant increase, but the ball was now rolling, and nothing could stop it. The additional $10 million appeared magically, through reprogramming from some already existing funding source. I never did find out how it was done, however, it seemed easy, given the history of the program.

One Last Hurrah

Although the Hush House structures were unlikely to be moved, moveable 'Equipment' required an 'Erection and Maintenance Manual,' which included three-dimensional drawings of parts and assembly drawings showing how the parts fitted together. Even the procedures for assembly, including crane location and equipment placement were required in the documentation. To keep the cost of all these drawings from getting out of hand, we convinced the Air Force to accept photographs showing the parts and assembly sequence. I was re-engaged to prepare the 'E and M' (Erection and Maintenance) manual, photographing parts and writing a description of the assembly process.

Deep In The Heart Of Texas

In January of 1981 Betty and I moved to San Antonio for about six months, so I could be on the job site every day, documenting the assembly of the first Hush House piece-by-piece. We packed everything we thought we would need into a two-door sedan and embarked on what we considered to be a sort extended camping trip.

After a two-day run down I-35W, we arrived in San Antonio and found that Copeland (sunglasses, right) was well into the Military Construction Phase. He had prepared the site, set forms and begun pouring concrete. Building above the foundations had not yet started, which gave Betty and me time to search for an apartment and get our living arrangements settled. We found an apartment on Evers Road, in NW San Antonio and rented enough furniture to make a comfortable accommodation. It was somewhat better than camping out; the place even had a small den, which served as an office.

San Antonio Construction Site

Computers and software weren't what they are now, and a word processor was a stand-alone device about the size of an office desk. They were also expensive —about $10,000. That was a lot more money in 1981 than it is now but essential for the job ahead. I bought one with a written agreement it would be repurchased from me in six months. It was fortunate I had a signed agreement; at the end of the term the rental company didn't really want it back. Technology moved fast; it was obsolete.

The job became mostly a routine: Turn up early on the job site, take pictures all day, drop the day's film off for processing and pick up yesterday's photos. After dinner, it was into the office to transcribe the day's notes and continue my narrative based on yesterday's pictures. It started with details: components and bolted joints. Eventually, we got into the assembly of major sub-structures and high work using cranes. The montage on the following page gives some flavor of the activity, but nobody wants a play-by-play of building one of these things except the Air Force. Even they are unlikely to dismantle one and reassemble it in a new location. In the end however, it was not a permanent building but an *'Equipment'* item, and it needed a manual.

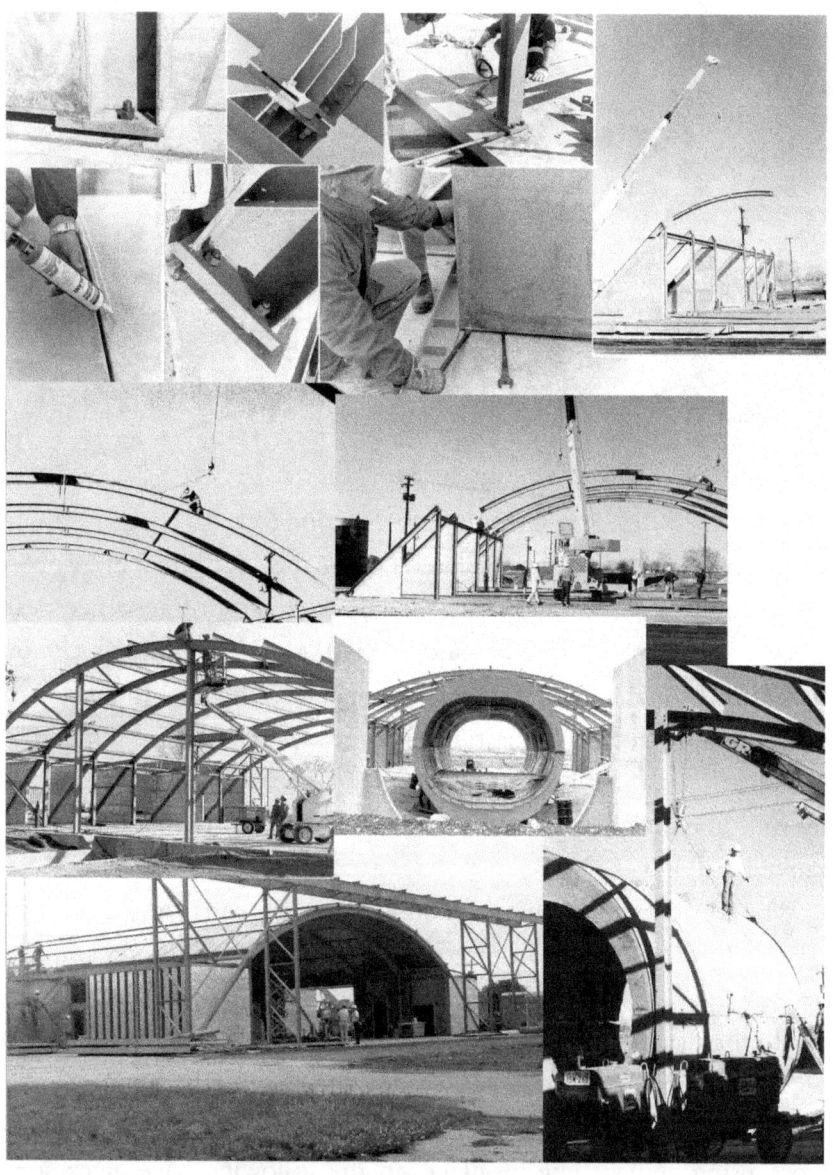

Construction Montage

Big Day

Finally, the SAALC crews began checkout of the facility with the full inventory of USAF airplanes and engines. I was determined to get an aerial view of the McDonnell-Douglas F-15, then the most advanced fighter in the inventory, as it was positioned in the facility for the first time. The Air Force personnel promised to have a helicopter available for a photograph of the occasion, but it never appeared – not unusual given all the program's earlier adventures. After almost four year's effort, however, I wasn't going to be denied this simple satisfaction.

First Hush House Occupant: McDonnell-Douglas F-15

I looked at the large construction crane, with its 80+ foot boom, and found a solution to my problem. I asked if anyone had a Bosun's Chair available. There was none. With a one-inch diameter hemp hawser, I fashioned a loop and dropped it over the crane hook, found a length of smaller rope to serve as a tag line, and tied it to my ankle. With a little help from the ground crew, this would keep me from rotating in the wind. I gripped the camera with one hand while holding on to the overhead rope to prevent falling out of the loop sling. Signaling 'up' to the crane operator, I was off. Success! (See inset in the photo, prior page).

But there was to be one last snag. About half-way up to the top of the boom, I was seized with intense pain in my lower leg. Balancing precariously in my rope sling, I instinctively lifted my pant leg above my calf-high boot and saw I was bleeding profusely. Changing my grip to better hold the camera and maneuvering for a closer look, I discovered a swarm of fire-ants, gnawing away at my leg between the boot-top and my knee. While I was being set up for the trip to the top of the crane, I had unfortunately been placed over a nest of these little devils, and I now learned first-hand that they can do a lot of damage in a very short time. It had taken only a few seconds for them to crawl to the top of my boot and go to work. By hanging the camera around my neck and shifting my grip once again, I was able to give the offenders a quick trip to the ground and proceed with the photo-shoot.

The Sell-Off

Proving the facility met specifications and was compatible with the required airplanes and bare engines in the Air Force inventory, is a process commonly referred to as 'Selling-off' the system. This involves collecting all the special tools, the restraint harnesses and other small details and checking to assure the facility met all the idiosyncrasies of each airplane or engine to be tested.

The key man in this was a technician, Jerry Hill, whom Copeland hired just after Hill retired from the Navy. He was a middle-aged man but appeared much younger. It was hard to imagine he was a 20-year veteran. Hill was quick-witted, always upbeat and could solve, innovate or adapt a fix for just about any electrical, mechanical or instrumentation problem that arose. He was also good at dealing with people, particularly the big brass types, who appeared frequently during construction. He refused to let them intimidate him — and they tried.

I got to know Hill pretty well. The nature of the job meant we spent a lot of time together, shared lunch hours, and occasionally we invited him to dinner and an evening at our apartment. Hill never spoke about his home, origins or family but frequently spoke of the Navy and his experience in the service of our country. Curious about his age and his time in the service, I asked him directly when the opportunity presented itself,

"Hill, how did you wind up in the Navy?"

"That's a bit of a story," he replied. "You see it's like this. I was 17 and living in a small Mormon community in Utah. My old man was a pillar of the town and an elder in the local Mormon Temple. I was a rake-hell, an embarrassment, and always in some sort of trouble. One night, on a dare from my girlfriend, I drove up main street in this little town, at 100 mph with a half-empty fifth of booze resting between my legs. My girlfriend was all over me, wearing nothing but a fully open blouse, no underwear and nothing except her shoes. My buddy was in the back seat with another girl; I didn't know what they were doing and didn't care.

"The local constable, an older gentleman whom I knew well and who knew my family, swung in behind me for a chase. With red light flashing, he gave it a serious try, but he was waaay behind. Given the speed we were going, he didn't have a chance, but it was no use to try to escape. He knew our family car, and I finally summoned enough sense to know I'd be arrested regardless and probably do jail time. I kept the speed up and outran him, until I was able to swing the bottle of booze over the top of the car and into the underbrush, unseen. Then I slowed down, pulled to the side of the road and waited. He stopped behind me and slowly got out of his car. The old constable, still shaking from the high-speed chase, directed a big flashlight in my eyes and recognizing me said,

"'C'mon, we're going to see your old man. Follow me, and I want you at the Justice of the Peace's Office at 09:00 in the morning.' My buddy and his girlfriend never even stopped doing whatever they were doing. I drove slowly back to town with a police escort, the only one I ever had. The old constable escorted me home, and when my dad opened the door, the constable said,

'I want you and this young man at the Justice's office at nine in the morning' and departed. My dad said only,

'You go to bed,' and he drove my friends home. I didn't sleep a lot that night.

"The next morning, my old man and I were at the JP's chambers at 09:00 sharp. The constable was already there. There were no lawyers, no harsh words, and no charges made or denied, in fact, no words at all. When the JP entered it was very formal, black robe and all. We rose and stood before him as he read the constable's report. It didn't take long; my reputation was well known. Finishing, the judge peered over the top of his glasses, looked me squarely in the eye and said,

'Young man, which branch of the service would you like to go into?' I didn't like walking, hated mud and dirt and knew the Navy carried plenty of its own food. Without further thought, I replied,

'Navy.' The following day my dad and I drove into Salt Lake and he signed permission for me to enlist, since I was under-age."

Hill was a really good man, and he was indispensable in the sell-off. The Navy did its job well. The fit and capability checks went well, thanks to Hill and his ingenuity.

13

The Calibration

Managed by a clown, it became somewhat of a circus.

* * *

Engine testing facilities are subject to periodic calibration, to as-sure tests conducted throughout the world are all rationalized in such a way as to give consistent results in any facility. This involves testing each facility against a cadre of 'gold plated engines,' a nickname for engines selected by the engine manufacturer as a representative standard of the type. They are then carefully treated, preserved and minimally run. A 'gold plated' engine 25 or 30 years old might have only a few tens of hours of operation in its record. Between tests, they are stored in hermetically sealed containers, and carried about the world in a C-130 cargo plane to ensure minimal wear and abuse.

The calibration of the Hush House began with the arrival of a load of 'gold-plated' engines one morning in late June. The engines were placed in storage to await the arrival of test personnel, from Tinker Air Force Base in Oklahoma City. From the outset, the facility calibration was not to be a happy experience.

Late one evening, while checking the facility, I noticed some new instrumentation was installed in the Hush House control room. There was no one else was around., but I took particular note of a mechanical, absolute pressure gauge of well-known precision man-ufacture, hanging on the control room wall. Its purpose appeared to be the measurement of barometric pressure.

*   *   *

A bit of description of the control room construction is in order. The control room is isolated from the testing area by thick walls, constructed with perforated metal face panels, packed between with basalt wool for acoustical isolation of the work area. The walls, while they appeared massive, allow air to freely pass through the acoustical material, although with some resistance to airflow. Since the control room is isolated from the test area by only these soft walls, the pres-sure in the control room is variable. It depends on whether the door to the outside is open or closed and/or the operating speed of the engine under test at any given moment. Thus, the pressure gauge on the wall read a 'barometric' value referenced to this variable pressure, rather than the true atmospheric pressure, as is common for aerodynamic measurements.

*   *   *

A terse sign was left on the desk, warning anyone who touches anything would be 'shot on sight.' It also contained the name, Jesse James, which matched the threat. The note also contained a hotel location and a phone number. I thought it only appropriate, to warn the writer about the structure of the control room and the measurement problem described above. I called the hotel.

The phone rang several times, and a voice rumbled gruffly,

"Jesse!"

"Mr. James?" I inquired.

"Yeah, whada ya want?" Perhaps I had interrupted a nap. I introduced myself and briefly described the structure and instrumentation problems associated with the Hush House control room.

"Listen," he responded, "I don't need no snot-nosed contractor to tell me how to do my job." I was taken aback, and after a short pause, I replied,

"OK, I'll see you at the job site tomorrow," and hung up the phone. It was not a good start.

The next day at the facility, Jesse avoided even eye contact and went about his test preparations, totally ignoring me. However, I noticed he had attached a pressure tube that led to the outdoors from the gauge in question, giving the gauge a proper reference to the atmosphere rather than the interior of the control room. However, he had also installed a bank of highly accurate liquid manometers along one wall of the control room, and they too were open to the control room environment with no outdoor reference. I didn't know how they would be used, and after the prior night's conversation, I elected not to inquire.

"Jesse"

Jesse was a study in himself. He was always fastidiously clean and neatly dressed in a workman's coverall suit he changed each day. The first day's suit was bright yellow in color, legs were cut well above the ankle and revealed matching, yellow socks. The coverall legs were sharply creased, at least early in the day.

What I didn't know, on first observation, was that he had at least six such coveralls: red, white, bright blue, green and orange, along with the yellow he was wearing. The legs on all were cut short, apparently deliberately, to highlight the socks.

He barked orders to his two minions. They were difficult for me to understand, until I noticed Jesse carried a gigantic quid of tobacco in his cheek. It appeared to be nearly half the size of a baseball, resulting in a sort of temporary speech impediment. On the job, at least, he was no Demosthenes. His two colleagues tried their best to emulate the boss, but they couldn't match the coveralls, only the quid of tobacco.

Jesse had forgotten more about running engines than I ever knew. He knew engines inside and out, but he didn't appear to understand basic physics of measurement. I said nothing further about measurement techniques, but I watched and waited to see what he was going to do with his bank of precision manometers. I was very curious to see how he would deal with the constantly changing pressure in the control room, to which one leg of his manometers was referenced. Although he had connected an outside atmospheric reference to the absolute pressure gauge, as I suggested, he apparently didn't appreciate that the open side of his manometers, also faced the continuously varying reference. As noted earlier, the operating speed of the engine under test and other variables, made the control room pressure useless as a reference.

I watched the initial run of the first engine he tested; it was a big one, either an F-100 or a J-75. As the day wore on, the runs became routine; I said nothing about Jesse's instrumentation.

In mid afternoon, while my attention was diverted talking to one of the workmen, there was a sudden explosion that shook the entire building. I ran for the control room, found the test-engine already winding down and asked what happened. Everyone in the room was silent. Then one of them quietly said to me, out of the side of his mouth and gesturing toward Jesse but behind his back,

"He closed the doors." I went out into the hangar area and looked at the multiple, roll-up doors. Their purpose was to block the spaces between the acoustic baffles, preventing dirt and varmints from entering, when the facility wasn't in use. More than half of them were closed, a strict no-no, but neither Hill nor I ever considered the possibility anyone might close them while running an engine. I returned to the control room and had a few words with Jesse. It was a loud, one-way monologue; Jesse said nothing. I told him, in no uncertain terms, he should concentrate on running his engines and we would run the facility. He wasn't to change any internal configuration detail, unless he talked to Hill or to me. Since he wouldn't speak to me, that meant Hill.

The explosion occurred because, with about half of the inlet doors closed, the large engine was able to draw only limited combustion and cooling air into the test area. It pumped the interior down to an unusually low pressure level. The lowered pressure, was ultimately relieved by higher-pressure air from outdoors rushing back upstream through the exhaust tube. Hill extracted from Jesse that the low pressure had exceeded "a little over six inches of water" on the manometer; one of the bystanders told me it was over 10. In any event, the structure of the facility had been thoroughly tested. Fortunately, the arch-shaped roof was more structurally capable than a flat one. However, at 10 inches of water equivalent pressure, the force on the flat front doors was about 30,000 pounds. The high-pressure 'whump' resulted when the suction force was suddenly released, creating an incalculable, reverse dynamic pulse on the doors. We were fortunate the doors didn't wind up lying on the concrete apron, but we survived the episode without damage. Jesse was no more communicative than before.

The Ultimate Crisis

For about three weeks, Jesse and his crew ground through his series of 'gold-plated' engines, dutifully filling all the little squares on their data sheets with numbers, gleaned from pressure measurements made with reference to an 'atmosphere' that was constantly varying. All data sheets carried the true atmospheric pressure as measured by the mechanical barometer that he had equipped with a tube extended to the exterior of the facility. However, the recorded measurements continued to be made, with all the manometers open to the interior.

The resulting error wasn't huge. A small reference manometer we located in the control room observation window, usually showed pressure difference, between the control room and the outdoors, of the order of one inch to two inches of water. This meant the measurements Jesse was making were as if an airplane or engine under test were at an altitude of about 70 to 130 feet above the actual elevation. Whatever the significance of the discrepancy, I could see no way to correct his data, since the reference pressure was changing with every different power setting of the engine. Because I didn't know the meaning of other pressures he was measuring in his system, I had no way of assessing the significance of the variable reference to those measurements.

On the final morning, we had only one engine left to complete the calibration. The testing continued longer than planned, and ASE Texas was badly in need of the funds to be released upon the official acceptance, which would follow the completion of the calibration tests. As the TF-41 engine spooled down, nearly four years of work on the Hush House wound down for me as well.

In a surprising gesture Jesse turned to me and flashed a big smile with his hand extended, simultaneously intoning,

"Good show!" They were the first words he had spoken to me since my telephone call to his hotel several weeks before. Then, drawing me away from the others in the control room, he attempted an apology, of sorts.

"You know," he began, mumbling through his large chaw of tobacco, "it would have worked out a lot better if we had started working together right from the beginning." I nodded agreement. Then he embarked on the real reason for his cordial approach.

"I've noticed," he continued, "that the little manometer you have in the control room window always reads different from mine." I was at a loss for words, but Jesse rescued me by continuing.

"I'd like to make one last run after lunch before we tear it all down. I'd like to compare your manometer readings with mine and see where the difference is." I replied,

"OK, we can do that. How about right after lunch?"

I hoped he hadn't seen my face turn ashen as I realized what this meant. At worst, we were looking toward a repeat of the whole gamut of engine tests. At best, we might calibrate the facility against our little $10 manometer and develop a correction factor, using the last remaining engine, but such a calibration would be engine specific. After observing Jesse for three weeks, I wasn't sure he understood the measurement process well enough to participate in an examination of the problem. Hill and I departed for a lunch by ourselves, so we could freely discuss our options.

I was ethically bound to attempt to explain to Jesse that he had a lot of questionable data. On the other hand, I knew ASE Texas was hurting financially and would be in a difficult position if the program were to be extended another three weeks. Hill and I talked about our options at length. There was no way we could see to correct the data analytically because Jesse had created a new science: *the science of variable constants*. Finally, I decided I'd have to discuss the whole data program with Jesse and attempt to assess how important the errors were. The altitude error was probably not a showstopper. Engines tested using Jesse's data were effectively at a higher reference altitude than the true test altitude and likely would produce more thrust than his measurements indicated if the data were reduced to 'standard day' conditions. I had no concept of the meaning of all the other measurements he made, but his data sheets showed him recording pressures to tenths of an inch of water pressure. The one to two inches of water pressure variations in the control room were 10 to 20 times the accuracies he considered important enough to record.

"I have to tell him, Hill," I said, finally.

"Let me handle it," Hill replied. "You haven't gotten along that well with him." I agreed.

When we arrived back at the facility, a C-130 cargo plane was already waiting for the last of its golden-engine cargo. All others had been loaded for the trip back to Oklahoma City, except for the TF-41, still on the thrust stand. There was real momentum rolling to finish the program and get out of town.

"I want to do a quick static pressure survey of the test area and compare your base manometer reading with mine," said Jesse. Hill fashioned a static pressure probe from a long length of tubing and a pole about 10 feet long, which would enable pressure measurements to be made at various levels in the test area. It was connected to both Jesse's manometers and our little reference manometer in the control room window.

I grabbed some ear protectors, and Jesse cranked his engine. He ran it at a variety of power settings while I walked about the test area, holding the makeshift pressure wand at various levels. Jesse and Hill were visible in the panoramic control room window, and each time I looked at them questioningly, both signaled a 'thumbs up.' I was puzzled and wondered what was happening. Finally, as the engine spooled down for the last time, I returned to the control room, trying to decide how I was going to approach the reference problem. Jesse informed me there was no difference between his instruments and ours. He turned away quickly, packaged his instrumentation in their luxuriously padded shipping containers and rolled the engine aboard the airplane. Before I could interrupt him, Jesse boarded the airplane without farewell greeting, the engines rolled and, the airplane taxied away.

Jesse was gone! It had been an orange suit day with orange socks, and I never had the courage to inquire about his possible ancestors.

As the C-130 lifted off and disappeared over the northern horizon, I turned to Hill and asked,

"Hill, what in the world happened in there?"

"It was pretty simple," Hill replied, "I took our little manometer from its place in the window, held it right in front of Jesse, removed the outdoor reference tube from it, even told him what I was doing, and how removing the tube would put our manometer to the same reference pressure as his. Then, I held the tube I removed right at chest level, in plain sight, during the entire survey you did of the test area. Of course, our manometer read the same as his; it then had the same reference pressure. I was pretty sure he didn't really understand what he was measuring anyway and took the chance he wouldn't get it." Intuitively, Hill understood people better than I did.

Given that episode, it would have been useless to challenge Jesse's measurement technique. He didn't appear to really understand the basics of manometry, and I wasn't eager to be called a snot-nosed contractor a second time. At least I managed to steer him into accurate measurement of each day's barometric pressure.

So, it was done. Almost four years had elapsed since I did the first theoretical analysis of the flow in a large ejector. Things had gone far afield from engineering. It had been quite a ride, and I was already off on another, overlapping odyssey in Canada, which would occupy much of my time for almost nine years.

Epilogue

The program had a somewhat sad ending beyond Olof Muten's untimely departure from the scene. While the first 25 Hush Houses were being completed, the Air Force was developing a second procurement to buy 80 more such facilities. Since they now owned the design and manufacturing rights, this was a completely normal procurement and competitive in every respect. All the old players were back in the competition and a few more as well. It would be a large and tough competition, likely exceeding $150 million in value.

My business arrangement with Olof was that I was be paid a retainer plus a contingent fee for my work, i.e. I gambled my time against the receipt of a very small fee, to be paid upon the successful signing of a contract. Initially, everyone concerned thought the ultimate program might result in a contract as large as $5 million, maximum. Now, there were some reservations regarding the payment of a consulting fee based on a follow-on program that would exceed $100 million. As a result, when I suggested we should attempt to position ASE Texas to repeat its success with the original 25 systems, they decided to work the problem without my help. They lost the 80-item procurement by less than 3%.

I don't think anyone but Olof appreciated the extent of the maneuvering required to land a contract of this size. As any farm boy knows, the hogs at the trough do a lot of pushing and shoving at feeding time; it's a tough game.

While ASE Texas faded away after the completion of the initial contract, it was very beneficial for the parent company, ASE in Saint Paul. As a result of the work on the Hush Houses, ASE emerged from a financial position of negative net worth and survived to acquire several higher technology companies in the Twin City area, where it thrives today.

*   *   *

Olof Muten died of other natural causes a few years after his riding accident and probably without any real understanding that we finally succeeded in fulfilling his personal wager of a lifetime.

Lars Broberg was found stiff and cold, still sitting at his desk at ASE in the mid-2000s.

John Copeland succumbed to the lure of the grape, and I'm told he drank himself into oblivion in the late 1990s – unverified.

I've lost track of Hill; he was one of those people who came into my life at a critical time but was on a train just passing through.

Paul Dembling remained a lifelong friend until he joined the innumerable caravan in his 90s. He retired and lived out his last years in Florida. We exchanged emails frequently until his email address went dark in 2013.

Sergeant Morris corresponded with me for several years after the Hush House program was completed. In his last letter, he informed me he had been diagnosed with Hodgkin Disease. Then the letters stopped. Sadly, I have no way of knowing his fate. An old cliché says, 'the good die young.'

The Buyer assigned to the program at San Antonio ALC, who battled me for nearly two years, all the way to the formation of ASE Texas, sought me out on one of my later visits to the Center to extend his hand and say,

"Hey, congratulations, no hard feelings. It was our general versus your general, and your general won." It wasn't quite that way, but his explanation will suffice, for now.

Appendix

The Procurement and Budgeting Process

Some wag once said our most potent weapon of war would be to introduce our enemies to the Department of Defense procurement system.

* * *

Overview and Some history

The most powerful force in the U.S. Government is money. The power inherent in its distribution drives the interest in perhaps the most sought-after jobs in Congress: the Chairmanships of the House of Representatives and Senate Budget Committees. Money is power. Power positions potentially comparable to these Chairmanships might be the Chairs of the Ways and Means Committee or the Rules Committee of the House of Representatives. The Rules Committee decides on the rules of debate in the House.

In the case of controversial programs of grand scale or importance the Chairman of the Rules Committee may decide, or at least influence, whether such a program will even come up for consideration in the House. But we are not speaking of grand programs here, just rather relatively minor endeavors, buried in the ultimate budget document and of a size that would almost be a rounding error in the programs that make daily news.

Historically, the budget committees are all-powerful and played a heavy-handed game in determining money flows from the final budget. The Chairman treated the final budget, as passed by both houses of Congress, as sort of spending guideline. The money allotted to a particular program in the line-itemized budget, might be 'adjusted' up or down, at the Chairman's discretion, or another small program inserted without passing through the authorization process. Thus, the Chairmanship is truly an all-powerful position with significant opportunity for chicanery.

Some decades ago, an attempt was made to remedy this 'hole' in the process, with the creation of the 'Authorization Committees' in both houses of Congress. In order to be considered in the final budget bill, an item had to pass an entirely separate screen: the 'Authorization Bill' that determines which programs are approved for consideration in the final 'Budget Bill.'

Thus, in addition to the many preliminary steps one has to endure to get a program funded, a major hurdle was added.

Confrontation

While the Authorization process was effective to a degree, it set the scene for confrontation, the intensity of which depended on the then-current occupants of the Chairmanships of Authorization and Budget Committees. The Budget Committees were resentful from the outset, bridling under the shadow of Authorization and remain so today. The attitude of the Budget Chairman might be, 'Go ahead, spend the money; it's approved in the Budget (even if it was never 'authorized'). This is the way we've done business for 200 years, and we're not going to change now.' The Chairman of Authorization might reply,

'You can't spend money that way; it hasn't been authorized.' The fight goes on today with ever-varying ferocity.

Shepherding a program through the entire process can be arduous, especially a program that has been inserted into the budget irregularly. Mostly, everyone looks away without challenging a stray dog – out of deference to colleagues – unless the grand total of such outlays exceeds some arbitrarily-perceived limit:

"We have more than a billion dollars of these 'adjusted' programs this year and it has to stop," might come the whine from Authorization sources.

The government buying process something is akin to sausage being made; it's hard to watch and even harder to explain. It is an elaborate process that strives (not too successfully) for the efficient purchase of devices and systems to satisfy needs of government entities at the operational level. These needs are assembled into a massive list, roughly rank-ordered in relative importance and matched to an estimate of the size of the current year's budget. Needs, of course, are always larger than the estimated funds available, so as the list is evaluated, a line is drawn through the ordered list, where the accumulated value of the individual items equals the money anticipated to be available. The objective of an advocate for a particular item is to make sure your project doesn't *fall below the line.'* The line becomes the world you live in.

Street Fighting

If your project falls 'below the line' you attempt to get it moved up the list. Generally, this isn't a matter of just getting it incrementally above the line but rather of arguing, 'well this is certainly more important than that.' The objective is to pick a vulnerable item, far enough up in the list to place your project out of vulnerability range of someone else, trying to do the same thing to you. It's a chaotic process with some rancor and sometimes chicanery. Positions in the list can change in the dark of the night, literally. It helps if you have some knowledgeable compatriot positioned to follow this process daily, if not hourly, as deadlines near.

In the case of the Air Force, much of this maneuvering is done by the Air Staff in the Pentagon. This is just the Air Force; at the same time the Army, Navy, Coast Guard, and other military organizations are going through a similar process. Beyond the Pentagon, the Departments of Agriculture, Education, social programs and all the governmental agencies, which make the evening news programs, are preparing lists that eventually wind up with the House of Representatives and Senate Authorization Committees who meld all these components into their respective master lists. Once again, you don't want your pet program to fall below the line in the grand list that becomes the heart of the Authorization Bill that is voted on by the entire assembly.

Just to make the process more interesting, after all the maneuvering and voting is finished, the House and Senate Authorization Bills may not be identical down to the last jot and tittle. The list of 'authorized' items must then be reconciled 'in committee,' an assembly of House and Senate members who debate together the fate of those items not identically described in one or the other of the final bills. The trick, for an individual advocate of a program, is to make sure the program of interest is *precisely* written into both the House and Senate bills so it doesn't '*come up in Committee*,' where it is subject to capricious action out of one's control. In the end, the two bills must be identical, and the final, reconciled bill is returned to the respective bodies, where it is passed in a final vote in each house.

Play It Again Sam

Perhaps you think that's certainly the end of the story. Well, it's not. Now we must do it all over again. When the final reconciled 'Authorization Bill' is ready for consideration to be included in the current year's Budget Bill, and the battle begins again. The estimated funding to be available is likely different, and the two Budget Committees may take different views of the itemized priorities to be considered in the final budget. As a result a whole new series of reordered lists and red lines that one's projects must not fall below. The fundamental process outlined above for Authorization is repeated, with additional opportunities for mischief. Is it any wonder the passage of the Budget Bill, in any given year, is usually late and voted upon in the wee hours of fiscal year's end? The power of the budget is nearly absolute and is the source of the prestige attached to being appointed to the budget committees of either the House or the Senate. The Chairman of either is akin to the Deity, and there is often real animosity between the Authorization and the Budget Committees.

As noted earlier, the Authorization process was inserted into the process by the whole Congress, in relatively recent times, to thwart the powerful manipulations of the two Budget Committees and is highly resented by both. Some would argue that *Authorization* has been only partially successful.

The Budget Committees tend to regard the Authorization process as guidance only. They seem to have regard only for the final amount approved in the Budget and may indulge in further manipulation of individual items contained in the larger collection. They may change the order of precedence presented in the Authorization Bill and even substitute unauthorized programs into their Budget Bills at the last moment. Budget Committees continue to sing a song of the ages:

"This is the way things have been done for 200 years, and we're gong to continue the process." It continues, with some limitations that result from the Authorization Process.

About The Author

Richard J. (Dick) Reilly grew up in a small, Southern Minnesota, rural town named after a Sioux Indian Chief, 'Hokah.' After primary and secondary education in local schools, he enrolled in the Aeronautical Engineering program at the University Minnesota, receiving a Bachelor of Science degree in 1951. After two years of post-graduate work, he began a professional career that spanned the aeronautical sciences, including basic research in boundary layer flow, high altitude research using free-flying balloons and engineering flight test work on general aviation airplanes, supersonic military aircraft and instrumentation for the U.S.'s first manned space flight.

He worked within corporate structures for 18 years, then began a consulting career based largely on the aeronautical sciences and reaching across five continents. Clients included a variety of corporate, international and government organizations, including the Advisory Group for Aerospace Research and Development (NATO), NASA and as guest lecturer at MIT, Penn State University and at universities of most of the NATO countries.

Reilly holds 16 patents in the general areas of aerodynamics, fluid power, control systems and computing devices.

www.ingramcontent.com/pod-product-compliance
Lightning Source LLC
Chambersburg PA
CBHW070859180526
45168CB00005B/1874